Counsel one another:

A Theology of Personal Discipleship

Paul Tautges

© Day One Publications 2009
First printed 2009

ISBN 978-1-84625-142-9

British Library Cataloguing ivn Publication Data available
Unless otherwise indicated, Scripture quotations taken from the New American Standard Bible®, Copyright
© 1960, 1962, 1963, 1968, 1971, 1972, 1973, 1975, 1977, 1995 by The Lockman Foundation Used by
permission. (www.lockman.org)
All rights reserved.

Published by Day One Publications
Ryelands Road, Leominster, HR6 8NZ

☎ 01568 613 740 FAX 01568 611 473
email—sales@dayone.co.uk
web site—www.dayone.co.uk
North American e-mail—usasales@dayone.co.uk
North American web site— www.dayonebookstore.com

Printed by Gutenberg Press, Malta

Endorsements

This book gets it right! Comprehensive and convincing, Counsel One Another *shows how true biblical counseling and preaching fit hand-in-glove. Those who preach, teach, or counsel regularly are sure to benefit greatly from this helpful resource.*

> **Dr. John MacArthur, pastor-teacher of Grace Community Church, Sun Valley, California; author; and Bible teacher on the** Grace to You **radio program**

Paul Tautges' book is readable, accessible, practical, and biblical. More than just a handbook for Christian counselors, Counsel One Another *encourages and enables the church to address the need for biblical discipleship. Loaded with information and application, this is an excellent workbook for all Christians who are seeking to grow in grace and take their rightful place in the body of Christ.*

> **Dr. Jim Winter, UK pastor for over twenty-five years, international lecturer, and author of** Opening up Ecclesiastes, Depression: A Rescue Plan, **and** Travel with William Booth

A gathering storm surrounds the day in which we live, a dark hour in which the absolute sufficiency of the Scripture has come under attack. But how refreshing—and rare—to see a book like this that asserts the irresistible power of God's Word to develop true discipleship by the sovereign working of His Spirit. This is not a 'trendy book' like so many, blown about by the prevailing evangelical winds. Rather, here is an anchor for authentic ministry that will stimulate real spiritual growth in God's people. May the Lord set an open door before this book and use it to affect the lives of many.

> **Dr. Steven J. Lawson, Senior Pastor, Christ Fellowship Baptist Church, Mobile, Alabama; speaker; and author of many books, including** Famine in the Land, The Expository Genius of John Calvin, **and** Foundations of Grace

The ministry of counseling has for too long been relegated to the professional counselor. Paul Tautges brings the biblical command for discipleship right back to the local church and to all believers. He takes the word "counseling," a word often perceived as being for professionals only (and threatening to average church laymen), and helps to reduce that fear, encouraging believers to fulfill their responsibility by uniquely redefining this ministry biblically as *intensely focused and personal discipleship*.

Rather than send people who are struggling spiritually, socially, and emotionally to a limited group of professionals, Tautges makes the case theologically that all church members have the responsibility to disciple one another and restore hurting people. He makes it clear that it is not just pastors who are responsible for counseling, but it is a "one-another-ministry" for all who claim the name of Christ.

Counsel One Another *is a must-read for all pastors and believers who take Matthew 28 and discipleship in the local church seriously.*

Dr. Ron Allchin, NANC Fellow, Executive Director of the Biblical Counseling Center, Arlington Heights, Illinois, and author of Ripening Sonship

Like their pastors, most Christians have adopted a professionalized or psychologized view of counseling that naturally excludes uneducated laity. This is why I believe that this book, Counsel One Another, addresses a serious deficiency in the discipleship ministry of Christians within the church. It advocates a radical departure from the status quo and a return to an authentic personal ministry of the Word among Christians through discipleship counseling. It effectively lays the theological foundation for Christians regaining the New Testament priority of addressing personal soul troubles with biblical counsel.

Dr. John D. Street, Chair, Graduate Program in Biblical Counseling, The Master's College and Seminary, Santa Clarita, California

Dedicated to:
Dick and Pat Otte,
human instruments of God,
who not only pointed me to salvation in Jesus Christ
but, like Paul in Corinth, invested almost two years
of their lives teaching me the way of discipleship;
&
Jerry Bridges,
who has discipled me through his books
from my earliest days as a believer.

Counsel One Another is a
companion volume to Paul
Tautges' *Counsel your Flock*,
Ministering the Master's
Way series, 96pp, ISBN 978-
1-84625-154-2.

Contents

A word of thanks

First, I thank Jesus Christ my Lord who, by His sovereign grace, saved me out of sin and spiritual blindness by the power of His Spirit through His gospel in the spring of 1984 and then called me into the ministry. To God be all the glory, "who has saved [me] and called [me] with a holy calling, not according to [my] works, but according to His own purpose and grace which was granted [me] in Christ Jesus before all eternity" (2 Tim. 1:9).

I thank my faithful wife, Karen, for her steadfast love and encouragement for twenty-two years and counting, and for never complaining about being a pastor's wife. No one could be a more suitable helper for this difficult man. "Her children rise up and bless her; her husband also, and he praises her, saying: 'Many daughters have done nobly, but you excel them all'" (Prov. 31:28–29).

I thank my children, Ashley, Kenan, Taylor, Kailyn, Alaina, Anna, Kayte, Leta, and Nolan, for their cheerful obedience, encouragement, and desire to follow the direction of their parents—two sinners saved by grace but striving to live for Jesus in the power of the Spirit. "Behold, children are a gift of the LORD" (Ps. 127:3).

I thank the wonderful flock that God has called me to shepherd, Immanuel Bible Church in Sheboygan, Wisconsin, for their faithful love and support for seventeen years and counting. I am also grateful to my fellow leaders, especially Bradford Canterbury, who carried an extra ministry load during the four-month leave of absence the church insisted I take in order to complete this project. "For just as we have many members in one body and all the members do not have the same function, so we, who are many, are one body in Christ, and individually members one of another" (Rom. 12:4–5).

I thank all those who checked this manuscript in its early stages: Eric Liederbach, Amy Anderson, Linda Baalke, Debbie Baugniet, Ashley Tautges, Bill Shannon and John Snyder. I also thank my dissertation committee, Dr. Dave Coats, Dr. Gary Gulan, Brent Belford, and Dr. Dick Fellars. I would also like to thank Dr. John Street of the Master's College and Seminary, for being so gracious and kind in writing the Foreword to this book. "Love is kind" (1 Cor. 13:4).

I thank my brother-in-law and sister, Kurt and Jean Kielisch, for years of encouraging words and for the frequent use of their cottage on Green Lake in the early part of 2007. I will never forget the early mornings I sat at the dining-room table watching the waterfowl play while I wrote, and wrote, and rewrote. "As each one has received a special gift, employ it in serving one another, as good stewards of the manifold grace of God" (1 Peter 4:10).

I thank my hungry students in Russia, who first received this material in a full week of lectures at Samara Preacher's Institute in the cities of Krasnodar and Samara. I am grateful to Brad Klassen and his capable team for their faithful teaching and leadership in these two schools and for their willingness to allow me to teach with them. I thank God for Victor Simeonovich Ryagusov, pastor of Transfiguration Church in Samara, for his unwavering vision for the establishment of church-based preachers' institutes so that biblical expositors may become fruitful and multiply throughout the land of Russia. May their tribe increase! "Preach the word; be ready in season and out of season; reprove, rebuke, exhort, with great patience and instruction" (2 Tim. 4:2).

I thank the faculty and administration of two educational institutions, Calvary Bible College and Northland Baptist Bible College, for their investment in my life and ministry. "The things which you have heard from me in the presence of many witnesses, entrust these to faithful men who will be able to teach others also" (2 Tim. 2:2).

Last, but not least, I thank Jim Holmes of Day One Publications for not deleting my initial email inquiry but instead responding with grace and the willingness to consider this material for publication. I also thank Mrs. Suzanne Mitchell for her grace and skill as my editor. Both of these servants have encouraged my own growth in Christ by being living examples of Colossians 4:6: "Let your speech always be with grace, as though seasoned with salt, so that you will know how you should respond to each person."

Foreword

It is unfortunate that the idea of Christians counseling one another has largely fallen into disfavor in the contemporary church. If you were to admonish average born-again Christians with the responsibility of counseling others, the common excuse would often be, "I'm not a counselor! That's something for a credentialed professional with a special gift and a Ph.D." Counseling is not conceived as a significant aspect of personal ministry for individual Christians in the church. For them, counseling is complicated, private and messy, something reserved for the specialist. This sophisticated, often sullied job is not the type most Christians are anxious to pursue. Essentially, this attitude has greatly diminished the personal ministry of the Word of God and gravely weakened the church.

How has such a narrow and negative view of Christians counseling one another become so entrenched in the church? For many pastors, it begins in the seminary. Most pastoral counseling classes strictly train pastors so that they are ill-equipped to handle serious soul turmoil, much less teach others to do so. Theological training is insufficient to deal with refined layers of consciousness. Only a licensed psychotherapist has the educated insight to decipher the complexities of the psyche. When this occurs, a seminary has tacitly acknowledged that the Bible is at best a primitive psychology, insufficiently sophisticated in matters of the soul.

Additionally, many seminaries teach a truncated view of ministry. Pulpit preaching is the exclusive task of the pastor, not counseling. Many men go to seminary to learn how to preach sermons, not shepherd individual souls or train congregations to counsel. As long as a pastor can preach a good sermon, he is well equipped to pastor a church. Not only does this concept of pastoral ministry violate the discipleship ministry of the New Testament church (Acts 20:20, 31; Col. 1:28–29), but it is also a wrong view of preaching. Preaching today is often restricted to the delivery of homiletical sermons from a church pulpit. But the New Testament semantic range of the word (2 Tim. 4:2; "to preach," Greek *kerusso*) is much broader and encompasses the meaning of the personal preaching of the Word through counseling.[1] One-on-one counseling is one form of proclaiming or preaching the Word, other than the proclamation of the Word from a pulpit.

Like their pastors, most Christians have adopted a professionalized or psychologized view of counseling that naturally excludes uneducated laity. This is why I believe this book, *Counsel One Another*, addresses a serious deficiency in the discipleship ministry of Christians within the church. It advocates a radical departure from the status quo and a return to an authentic personal ministry of the Word among Christians through discipleship counseling. It effectively lays the theological foundation for Christians regaining the New Testament priority of addressing personal soul troubles with biblical counsel.

Dr. John D. Street
Chair, Graduate Program in Biblical Counseling
The Master's College and Seminary, Santa Clarita, California

Introduction

Chapter 1

The need for this book

Recent comments in an editorial in *The Wall Street Journal* testify to the church's growing confidence in Christian psychology as the answer to the church's need for the ministry of counseling. In this brief article entitled "Growing Christian Shrinks," Cara Marcano states, "Psychology is one of the 10 largest majors at the more than 100 schools that are members of the Council for Christian Colleges & Universities," according to the council's vice president.[1] The Christian interest in embracing psychology and religiously mixing it into a crock of therapeutic stew continues to rise. Hence, there is a need for a study of the type of counseling ministry that will benefit believers the most.

Ms. Marcano goes on to affirm that the most popular Christian psychologists "are still those who keep their faith separate from their discipline. [For example] David Myers, a professor at Hope College in Holland, Mich., and the author of a well-known introductory psychology text, is also a Christian. But he is hardly known as a Christian at all in most mainstream psychological circles."[2] The discerning believer is thus forced to ask how a Christian author can write a textbook on the science of human behavior and leave Jesus Christ out. How can a famous Christian psychologist not even be known as a Christian in his closest circle of influence? How can a psychology that is called "Christian" (*like Christ*) be indistinguishable from anything the rest of the world has to offer? No wonder Christian psychologists are so popular! The offense of the cross has been trumped by a greater love for social and intellectual acceptance, resulting in the man-centered theories of human behavior these psychological counselors promote being so readily received. The reason for this appears to be that these theories have been completely gutted of *true* biblical psychology—a worldview that exalts Jesus Christ as the perfect God-man, the crucified and risen Lord who came to save sinners from the penalty and power of indwelling sin.

The *Wall Street Journal* article rightly gives credit to Fuller Seminary, located in Pasadena, California, for pioneering the integration of psychology and theology. Fuller's "was the first clinical psychology program outside a university to receive accreditation from the American Psychological Association. Its model, which is increasingly popular at Christian colleges in the U.S., combines serious theological study with rigorous psychological training, promoting 'the cross in the heart of psychology.'"3 However, what the article could not even have begun to uncover is the root cause of Fuller Seminary's love affair with psychology; that is, its willful departure from sound theology, most particularly, its rejection of the inerrancy of Scripture, and the resulting loss of confidence in Scripture's authority and sufficiency for life. In a day when doctrinal compromise is all too common, the church's faith in the sufficiency of the Bible must be restored. A brief history lesson is in order.

The account of Fuller's doctrinal shift is astutely recorded by historian George Marsden in his intriguing book *Reforming Fundamentalism*.4 The book's subtitle, *Fuller Seminary and the New Evangelicalism*, indicates how one seminary's departure from its confidence in the Scriptures serves as an illustration of the change in Bible-believing Christianity in general. The primary goal of Charles Fuller and the other founders in 1947 was to establish a school of higher learning that would fill the void left by the loss of Princeton (and other institutions) to theological liberalism. Harold Lindsell, one of Fuller's four original faculty members, later wrote about the school's beginnings in his bombshell book on the war against inerrancy, *The Battle for the Bible*. In the chapter entitled "The Strange Case of Fuller Theological Seminary," Lindsell provides the following commentary on the school's beginnings: "He [Charles Fuller] and the founding fathers, including the founding faculty, were of one mind with respect to the Scriptures. It was agreed from the inception of the school that through the seminary curriculum the faculty would provide the finest theological defense of biblical infallibility or inerrancy."5 The desire of the founders was to create a place where both the evangelist and the scholar could be trained to offset the destruction caused by modernism. A highly intelligent faculty would also be given time to publish substantial theological works that would earn a level of respectability for the school and movement. In so doing, they believed they could create a New Evangelicalism that held firmly to the fundamental doctrines of Scripture, yet discarded the harsh spirit prevalent in cultural fundamentalism.

According to George Marsden, a big break came when Edward J. Carnell, one of Fuller's brightest theological minds, secured a book contract with a major secular publisher, which was considered "a great triumph for the new evangelicals."[6] However, the arrival of the book, *Christian Commitment: An Apologetic*, in 1957 was a significant shift away from the biblical, Christ-centered gospel toward a psychologized, man-centered message. According to Marsden, this original volume from Carnell's pen specifically "played down the gospel's offenses to secular culture."[7] In addition, his apologetic works in general were "conspicuous among evangelical literature in their relatively sparse references to Scripture."[8] This absence of the Word of God in his writings was intentional, as Carnell sought to persuade the unbelieving mind of the truth of Christianity not by appealing to the authority of Scripture, which unbelievers often scoff at, "but to truths derived from some common human experience."[9] Thus the way was prepared for human reason, based on experience, to eclipse the biblical gospel.

The subsequent downgrade from questioning the authority of Scripture to rejecting its sufficiency for life and godliness was no surprise. Though Fuller Seminary's original roots clung deeply to the authority of God's Word and the supremacy of the saving gospel of Christ, what became apparent only a decade after its founding was the snowball effect of theological compromise as the seminary's scholars "were now asking what they could learn from contemporary thought."[10] It quickly became apparent that faith in the authority of Scripture waned in direct proportion to their growing confidence in human philosophy.

Three years later, in 1960, Carnell published another work, *The Kingdom of Love and the Pride of Life*. Marsden notes that this book "was more modest, gentle, and artful than his other books. He had been reading Freud [1856–1939] and was impressed by the coincidence of the insights of modern psychology and what he himself was seeing more and more as the heart of the gospel." Therefore, "Christian apologetics, he argued ... must add to its repertoire an appeal to the universal need for love."[11] This may appear to have been merely a small addition to the Christian faith, but in reality it was an enormous step away from the heart of the biblical gospel. Instead of holding to the truth that man is utterly depraved and in need of God's gracious redemption, Carnell began to believe man's root problem was unmet psychological needs. Adding the teachings of Sigmund Freud to the teachings of Jesus Christ could result in nothing less than a departure from biblical truth, since Freud considered himself a savior whose purpose was to rescue people from the bondage of faith in God. Os Guinness writes, "It is well known that Freud dismissed religion as an 'illusion' and saw himself as a 'new Moses' with [Carl Gustav] Jung as his 'Joshua.' He advocated psychotherapy as 'a reeducation' for a new human civilization through a complete reversal of Mosaic morality and God-grounded objective guilt. Psychological liberty to Freud was a matter of messianic liberation."[12] Edward Carnell's digression from the Christ-centered gospel of Scripture to the man-centered gospel of Freudianism fits the scenario of Romans 1:21–22 perfectly. When men cease to honor God as God they become futile in their theories and their foolish hearts are darkened. The more they profess to having obtained human wisdom, the more they become fools. Therefore, it is to be expected that, when a church or seminary departs from the doctrine of inerrancy, a rejection of the Bible's authority and sufficiency will follow not long afterward. And once the authority and sufficiency of the Bible are undermined, it soon follows that belief in the total depravity of man and his desperate need of redemption through Jesus Christ is replaced by the psychological gospel of self-improvement.

Almost a decade after leaving Fuller Seminary, Harold Lindsell correctly predicted that the departure from the inerrancy of Scripture would "lull congregations to sleep and undermine their belief in the full-orbed truth of the Bible; it will produce spiritual sloth and decay; and it will finally lead to apostasy."[13] Man-centered wisdom wastes no time in filling the vacuum created by abandoning sound doctrine. As in the days of Jeremiah, they forsook God and shaped for themselves "cisterns, broken cisterns that can hold no water" (Jer. 2:13). In the case of Fuller Seminary, the road was now paved and the birth of a school of psychology was fast approaching.

However, before this graduate school could become a reality, several key players had to be put in place. Since news of doctrinal compromise at the school had begun to spread, many faithful supporters chose to withdraw their regular giving from the Fuller Evangelistic Foundation, a major source of income for the seminary from its birth, creating a significant funding obstacle. As a result, Marsden believes, "Unquestionably the most important addition to the board of trustees was C. Davis Weyerhaeuser," the lumber tycoon from Tacoma, Washington.[14] Weyerhaeuser's influence extended far beyond girding the school's financial situation since he too was waffling on the doctrine of inerrancy. In fact, according to Lindsell, the new board member made no bones about it. He "was clear in his own conviction that the Bible had errors in it. Nor did he hesitate to make his position plain."[15] Once elected as chairman of the board of trustees, Weyerhaeuser, along with the new dean of faculty Daniel P. Fuller and theistic-evolutionist J. Laurence Kulp, could advance the cause of "the progressive party," those campaigning for the removal of inerrancy from Fuller's creed.[16] Finally, after the progressive members of the faculty and the board of trustees succeeded in taking over the school and establishing their new order by forcing the inerrantists out, the field was tilled and ready to receive the planting of a school of psychology.

Relevant to the subject of counseling, however, is the interesting fact that the initiative to found a school of psychology "arose almost solely from Davis Weyerhaeuser and his wife Annette, who promised to finance the founding of the enterprise."[17] Marsden continues, "Annette Weyerhaeuser's role was central. She herself had suffered from some debilitating anxieties since early in their marriage."[18] With her having received help from a psychiatrist, the conviction was firmly established in the minds of this wealthy couple that what was most needed was a school that would specialize in the integration of theology and psychology. Thus, in 1965, the Fuller Graduate School of Psychology opened its doors. However, rather than establishing a ministry-based approach to counseling that was saturated with Scripture, "From the outset the founders envisioned the School of Psychology not as a center for pastoral psychology, but as a bona fide Ph.D. program in clinical psychology, to which they would add substantial theological perspectives."[19] (And "add" theological perspectives is exactly what they had to do, since psychology is fundamentally anti-God.)

Yet the founders' quest for integration could not be accomplished in a manner acceptable to a wider society without a nationally known figurehead. Subsequently, a search began for a psychologist who was respected enough by academia that his credentials and fame would help the new school "gain early accreditation."[20] The search ended when Lee Edward Travis agreed to take the post. Travis, "one of the leading figures in the history of American psychology,"[21] was a baptized Mormon who had fallen away from his church. After a forty-year absence from involvement in his religion, Travis began attending a Presbyterian church in southern California where "he found himself overwhelmed by a profound sense of transcendence in which he felt found by God."[22] As a result, only three years after his profession of faith in Christ, Dr. Travis agreed to take on the ground-breaking assignment which would shape the future of the New Evangelicalism. Marsden's comments concerning Travis's lack of theological grounding are invaluable:

> Although his interests were wide and his theological instincts sound by Fuller standards, he was a new Christian and first had to learn theology in order to talk about integration. While he took up this task with eagerness, his policy for the school itself was that it first had to excel by conventional standards in clinical psychology before it could expend its energies in the unexplored areas of theoretical integration. The theoretical explorations were thus an added-on part of the program.[23]

Thus it has always been for "Christian psychology" from its beginnings—a little theology here, a little theology there, built upon the faulty foundation of man's so-called wisdom. The enormous influence that Fuller Seminary has had in the field of counseling simply cannot be ignored. As in the book of First Corinthians, where the Apostle Paul confronts the church's shift away from the gospel to the false security of the wisdom of men (1 Cor. 1:21), this man-centered integrationism, pioneered by Fuller, cannot be left unchallenged.

The statement of the problem

In 1991, John MacArthur published a book entitled *Our Sufficiency in Christ*, in which he exposed three deadly influences within Christianity, one of which is "the infusion of psychology into the teaching of the church." He observes,

> There may be no more serious threat to the life of the church today than the stampede to embrace the doctrines of secular psychology. They are a mass of human ideas that Satan has placed in the church as if they were powerful, life-changing truths from God ... The result is that pastors, biblical scholars, teachers of Scripture, and caring believers using the Word of God are disdained as naïve, simplistic, and altogether inadequate counselors. Bible reading and prayer are commonly belittled as "pat answers," incomplete solutions for someone struggling with depression or anxiety. Scripture, the Holy Spirit, Christ, prayer, and grace—those are the traditional solutions Christian counselors have pointed people to. But the average Christian today has come to believe that none of them really offers the cure for people's woes.[24]

These words of a modern-day preacher echo the stern warning that God gave long ago through His prophet Jeremiah: "Cursed is the man who trusts in mankind and makes flesh his strength, and whose heart turns away from the LORD" (Jer. 17:5). Clearly, a man-centered philosophy of life is not the way to God's blessing. The widespread acceptance of integrationism in the ministry of counseling, therefore, is a major problem. This book counters the problem by replacing it with a biblical theology of discipleship that is truly God-centered.

The solution to the problem

Jeremiah not only warns against trust in man, because it leads away from God, but he also testifies concerning the blessing that is showered upon those who trust in God: "Blessed is the man who trusts in the LORD and whose trust is the LORD" (Jer. 17:7). This warning and promise raise important questions related to counseling: If a man-centered, psychological approach to behavioral change is not the way God intended for believers to be helped to conquer their personal problems, what, then, is the way? If the clinical counselor, trained in all the latest ever-changing theories of human motivation, cannot offer anything that is ultimately life-transforming, how are people to receive the help they so desperately desire? The solution remains the same now as it was in the days of the apostles: biblical counseling as a normal part of biblical discipleship.

The intended scope of this book

Believers in Jesus Christ must be taught and trained to be richly indwelt with the Word of God, to live under the influence of the Holy Spirit, to be driven by the gospel, to express dependence on God through prayer, to be motivated by love for God and neighbor, and to be moved with compassion to help one another make progress in the ongoing work of sanctification. This is authentic biblical counseling. Therefore, in this book, counseling will be presented as a targeted form of discipleship, an intensely focused and personal "one-another" ministry aimed at the serious development of serious disciples.

The next chapter establishes the biblical basis of counseling as the fulfillment of Jesus' great command to the church to make disciples who are obedient to the Word of God. Chapter 3 explains the challenge that man's depravity brings to the process of discipleship, focusing specifically on God's supernatural work of deliverance by conversion. Chapter 4 sets forth the indispensable requirement of personal discipline of the mind, heart, and life habits for the ongoing pursuit of godliness. Chapter 5 defends the need for compassion in the one-another ministry of restoration within the family of God. Chapter 6 puts in plain words the underlying conviction of authentic biblical counseling regarding the sufficiency of the Scriptures for life and godliness. Chapter 7 tackles the issue of psychological counseling by comparing the futility of man's wisdom with the supremacy of the wisdom of God as revealed by the Holy Spirit in the Word of God. Finally, Chapter 8 returns the ministry of discipleship counseling to its intended place—the Christ-centered, gospel-saturated local church that functions as a community of believers who are stimulating one another's faith toward the fullness of maturity in Jesus Christ.

The definition of key terms

The New Testament uses four different words to emphasize this more concentrated aspect of the disciple-making process: *parakaleo*, *protrepo*, *noutheteo*, and *paraineo*. The meanings and uses of these words help us to envision a well-rounded ministry that is geared toward helping people change.

First, according to *Vine's Expository Dictionary of Old and New Testament Words*, the Greek word *parakaleo* means "to call to one's side," hence, "to call to one's aid." It is used for every kind of calling which is meant to produce a particular effect, hence its various meanings such as "comfort, exhort, desire, call for."[25] The Apostle Peter uses this word to urge Christians to abstain from fleshly lusts (1 Peter 2:11), and the author of Hebrews insists that believers are to encourage one another to be faithful to their local assembly (Heb. 10:25). God's plan for personal character transformation has always included other persons in the community of the faith because normal spiritual growth does not take place in isolation, but rather alongside others.

Second, the Greek word *protrepo* means "to urge forward, to push on, to encourage."[26] For example, when Apollos desired to go to Achaia, the brethren "encouraged" others to welcome him with grace (Acts 18:27). Therefore, we will discover that, from time to time and in varying degrees, every person needs to be motivated to keep pressing forward in his or her pursuit of the application of biblical truth to life.

Third, *A Linguistic Key to the Greek New Testament* says that the Greek word *noutheteo* means to admonish or warn. It means to put before the mind so as to "correct through instruction and warning."[27] It differs slightly from teaching in that it is normally a response to some kind of error or it is a warning against spiritual danger, present or potential. When Paul counseled the Ephesian elders about the danger of the emerging false teachers who would seek to make disciples by their false doctrines, he reminded them of the three years in which he did not cease to admonish them (Acts 20:31). Romans 15:14 teaches that believers should be able to admonish one another biblically. This should always be toward the goal of spiritual maturity (Col. 1:28), and therefore believers should appreciate the shepherds who give them instruction toward that end (1 Thes. 5:12). The noun form, *noutesia*, means "training by word—either of encouragement, when this is sufficient, or of remonstrance, reproof, or blame, where required."[28] Therefore, we will also discover that God's plan for making disciples requires believers to care enough to confront one another when brothers or sisters they love are in error, and to firmly warn or instruct them concerning their spiritual danger.

Finally, the Greek word *paraineo* means "to admonish by way of exhorting or advising."[29] An example of this is when, in the midst of a storm at sea, Paul admonishes his fellow sailors and urges them to keep their courage (Acts 27:9, 22). Therefore, we will also discover that the process of spiritual growth requires believers to give courage to their fellow companions on the journey of discipleship, especially when they are in the midst of the storms of life.

In all these cases, these believers are "counselors," with or without a title. And the counsel dispensed is always in the form of words spoken from the commitment of biblical love. Proverbs 18:21 says, "Death and life are in the power of the tongue." As biblical counselors, we must take great care in the words we use with our disciples, for speech has the power to kill them with despair or to give them the hope of life. I appreciate David Powlison's simple definition of counseling as "intentionally helpful conversations."[30] The power of biblical counsel lies in the degree to which *our* words are filled with *the* Word.

The working definition

The definition that I will develop and defend throughout this book is as follows: Biblical counseling is an intensely focused and personal aspect of the discipleship process, whereby the more mature believer (counselor) comes alongside the less mature believer (counselee) for three main purposes: first, to help that person to consistently apply Scriptural theology to his or her life in order to experience victory over sin through obedience to Christ; second, by warning that person, in love, of the consequences of sinful actions; and third, by leading that person to make consistent progress in the ongoing process of biblical change in order that he or she too may become a spiritually reproductive disciple-maker. This definition describes the aim of biblical discipleship and supports the underlying principles of this book. Biblical counseling is helping one another, within the body of Christ, to grow to maturity in Him.

It has been said, "The faithful preacher will milk a great many cows, but he will make his own butter."[31] So it is with this book. Remembering every person, author, theologian, friend, or teacher who has influenced my thinking over almost two decades of involvement in the ministry of disciple-making is impossible. However, I have done my best to give credit to every "cow" that has given me "milk." Therefore, I trust the "butter" will be useful to the church that Jesus gave His lifeblood to redeem. "Worthy are You to take the book and to break its seals; for You were slain, and purchased for God with Your blood men from every tribe and tongue and people and nation" (Rev. 5:9).

For further thought and small-group discussion

1. Read Romans 1:16–32. Discuss the downward spiral that occurs when the truth of the biblical gospel is suppressed by man-centered wisdom.

2. Read Jeremiah 17:5–8. Discuss the differences between trusting man and trusting God, and the consequences of each.

3. Read Hebrews 10:24–25. Discuss the reasons why God calls believers in Christ to be faithful to help one another experience spiritual growth. Compare this priority with the Apostle Paul's approach to ministry as explained in Colossians 1:28.

4. Read Romans 15:13–14. What role does God want you to have in the lives of other believers?

5. Read Proverbs 18:21; Colossians 4:6; and Ephesians 4:29. Discuss the power of language. What changes does the Holy Spirit want you to make in your manner of speech toward others?

The content of the Great Command

Chapter 2

But the eleven disciples proceeded to Galilee, to the mountain which Jesus had designated. And when they saw Him, they worshiped Him; but some were doubtful. And Jesus came up and spoke to them, saying, "All authority has been given to Me in heaven and on earth. Go therefore and make disciples of all the nations, baptizing them in the name of the Father and the Son and the Holy Spirit, teaching them to observe all that I commanded you; and lo, I am with you always, even to the end of the age."

–Matt. 28:16–20

Authentic biblical counseling is nothing more, and surely nothing less, than the fulfillment of the Great Command to make disciples of Jesus Christ by the delegated authority of God and the empowerment of the Holy Spirit. God's vision of discipleship requires that we view any and every ministry we may call "counseling" as an essential part of the overall means of shepherding people toward submissive faith in Jesus Christ as Lord and Savior and training them to walk in daily obedience to His Word. Therefore, we must consciously use the terms *counseling* and *discipleship* interchangeably, or even together (*discipleship counseling*), in order to communicate that counseling is not the specialized ministry of a few professionals, but rather an intensely focused, personal aspect of the discipleship process for all believers. That is, it is disciple-making targeted at specific areas of a person's life where biblical change is needed for that follower of Christ to move forward toward the goal of being fully remade into His likeness.

In a way, the "rediscovery"[1] of biblical counseling among Christians is evidence that intentional discipleship has for too long been a missing link in the church. Bill Hull, in the first chapter of his book *The Disciple Making Pastor*, writes,

> I have thrown down the gauntlet. I maintain that the evangelical church is weak, self-indulgent, and superficial, that it has been thoroughly discipled by its culture. As Jesus said, "When a disciple is fully taught, he will be like his

teacher" (see Luke 6:40). Furthermore, I believe the crisis of the church is one of product, the kind of people being produced. I propose the solution to be obedience to Christ's commission to "make disciples," to teach Christians to obey everything Christ commanded.[2]

Thus, what is most commonly referred to as the Great Commission is, in this book, called the Great Command—a title that keeps the general command consistent with its specific content. Obedience to Christ is the very heart of the content of our marching orders. *Obedient* describes the product we are called to reproduce. In other words, the word *command* communicates the authority given to the church and also the directives to be obeyed by both disciple-makers and those being discipled so that more and more sinners are redeemed by the gospel of Jesus Christ and become His obedient followers.

Analysis of disciple-making

In order to demonstrate that authentic biblical counseling is a matter of fulfilling our God-given command to make disciples, we must begin with a biblical understanding of discipleship itself. To do so, we must define two terms: *disciple* and *discipleship*.

WHAT IS A DISCIPLE?

The Great Command at the end of Matthew's Gospel contains one main action: "make disciples" of Jesus Christ (28:18–20). But what is a disciple? A disciple (*mathetes*) is "one who follows one's teaching … not only a pupil, but an adherent."[3] This is probably why F. Wilbur Gingrich chose the word "apprentice."[4] Therefore, a disciple of Jesus Christ is not merely one who confesses Christ, though that certainly is true (Rom. 10:9), but one who intentionally attaches him- or herself to Him[5] and adheres, or submits, to His commands as the new standard for living, and consequently becomes like Him. There can be no doubt that this is exactly what Jesus means in Luke 6:40: "A pupil [*mathetes*] is not above his teacher; but everyone, after he has been fully trained, *will be like his teacher*."[6] Edward Hinson explains Jesus' concept of a disciple this way:

> In the ancient world a "disciple" was a person who became totally disciplined to the life of his master-teacher. He shared the master's life-message as well as his didactic message. Jesus required His disciples to abide in His word (John 8:31), meaning they were not only to listen to His message, but to adopt it as

their way of life. To the ancient Greek the disciple was bound to his master by the ideas of the teacher, whereas, to the Jewish disciple, he was bound to the rabbi by his knowledge of the law (Torah). In contrast to both, Jesus (cf. John 6:64) bound His disciples to Himself! ... Since it is Christ who decides who will enter discipleship, it is also He who lays down the conditions for discipleship. They obey His words because of their commitment to Him personally and renounce all material comforts which may hinder their allegiance to Him (Matthew 10:37) ... A "disciple" (*mathetes*) is synonymous with a "servant" of Christ. Thus, a disciple has bonded himself willingly to the Master-Teacher for a lifetime relationship ... The disciple does not attempt to make Christ his Lord through a lifelong struggle. Christ is already his Lord, and he must learn to obey Him as such.7

A disciple of Jesus Christ is one who is committed to a lifelong process of growing in obedience to his Master's commands and, by doing so, becomes like Him.

What is discipleship?

Jesus' command to His followers was nothing short of a mission of spiritual reproduction. The verb form of *mathetes* means "to instruct with the purpose of making a disciple. *Matheteuo* must be distinguished from the verb *matheo* (which is not found in the NT), which simply means to learn without any attachment to the teacher who teaches. *Matheteuo* means not only to learn but to become attached to one's teacher and to become his follower in doctrine and conduct."8 In other words, the task of the church is to lead others not merely to acknowledge the Son of God as having come in the flesh in the person of Jesus Christ (though that is an essential point in a doctrinal system that is truly biblical; see 1 John 4:2–3), but to lead them to become submissive Christ-followers who are willing, by faith, to live and die for Him and for His message. In his classic work, *The Master Plan of Evangelism*, Robert Coleman describes how the first disciples reckoned with the reality of Jesus' call to obedience, explaining that

> following Jesus seemed easy enough at first, but that was because they had not followed Him very far. It soon became apparent that being a disciple of Christ involved far more than a joyful acceptance of the Messianic promise: it meant the surrender of one's whole life to the Master in absolute submission to His sovereignty. There could be no compromise.9

This is the honest reality of being a true disciple and, therefore, the church must take the initiative to pursue a biblical approach to ministry that will produce believers who live in obedience to Christ.

My point is simply this: the content of the Great Command demands a commitment to biblical counseling since discipleship is the very core of counseling. Counseling that is merely therapeutic massaging of the bothered soul is not counseling as God defines it. True biblical counseling is that which functions within relationships which exist as fruit of the ongoing command to make disciples of Jesus Christ by moving others farther down the road of obedience to His Word. Jim Berg rightly asserts, "Biblical discipleship is not primarily a program. It is a certain kind of *relationship ... Discipleship is helping another believer make biblical change toward Christlikeness*—helping others in the sanctification process."[10] To accomplish this, the risen Christ delegated His authority to carry out actions consistent with the goal of making obedient followers, while assuring us of His continued presence.

Authority for disciple-makers

It is important to note that Jesus promised His authority because "some were doubtful" (Matt. 28:17). That is, some of His followers questioned whether or not He who met them on the designated mountain was truly the same Jesus who had earlier been arrested and murdered in their presence. Therefore, the resurrected Christ backed up His Great Command with divine authority to carry it out: "All authority has been given to Me in heaven and on earth" (v. 18). "All authority" refers to "every form of authority; [the] command of all means necessary"[11] to carry out the commission. In short, our God-given resources are sufficient for this enormous task.

Shortly before His arrest, Jesus lifted up His eyes to heaven and prayed, "Father, the hour has come; glorify Your Son, that the Son may glorify You, even as You gave Him authority over all flesh, that to all whom You have given Him, He may give eternal life" (John 17:1–2). The same authority that the Father delegated to the Son to grant salvation to those whom God had chosen was now being delegated to followers of Jesus to fulfill the Father's sovereign promise to His Son—to produce a flock of Christ-followers.

God's authority is inherent in His nature—He is God! Our authority, on the other hand, is delegated; it is received from the One who in Himself possesses the right to command others. This delegation of authority is essential in light of two realities: the obedience of the gospel and the opposition of Satan.

AUTHORITY IS ESSENTIAL BECAUSE OF THE GOSPEL

First, Scripture never presents the gospel in the manner in which it is frequently offered to people today—as an option, as something to be believed by those who want a better life whenever they choose. In reality, the gospel is a message that God *commands* us to believe. The Apostle Paul cites this truth as the basis of God's judgment of unbelievers: "the Lord Jesus will be revealed from heaven with His mighty angels in flaming fire, dealing out retribution to those who do not know God and to those who *do not obey the gospel* of our Lord Jesus" (2 Thes. 1:7–8). The Apostle Peter teaches the same. When urging believers to joyfully suffer for righteousness instead of complaining about self-inflicted suffering caused by our own foolishness, he says, "For it is time for judgment to begin with the household of God; and if it begins with us first, what will be the outcome for those who *do not obey the gospel* of God?" (1 Peter 4:17). The Apostle John writes, "This is His *commandment*, that we *believe* in the name of His Son Jesus Christ" (1 John 3:23).

Understanding the gospel as a command to be obeyed has radical implications for discipleship. As we counsel others, we have a divine obligation to make it clear that believing in Christ is not an option—we *must* believe. God commands trust in Christ alone as the One who saves us from the just display of God's wrath (Rom. 5:9). This is the only acceptable response from sinners. Therefore, we must use our delegated authority from Christ to tell sinners that they *must* believe the gospel. Believing in Christ then begins a new life of submission to His will.

Not only must we understand the gospel as God's command to sinners, but also, as regenerate disciple-makers, we must recognize that teaching the gospel is a command that we must continually obey. In his opening words to the believers in Rome, the Apostle Paul makes it clear that he cannot be faithful to God without preaching the gospel. He considers himself a "bond-servant of Christ Jesus, called as an apostle, set apart for the gospel of God" (Rom. 1:1). The gospel (*euangelion*) is the glad tidings of Jesus to which God separated Paul. The message of the Scriptures concerning Jesus Christ, therefore, became Paul's preoccupation because he understood that God made him a steward of the gospel in order "to bring about *the obedience of faith* among all the Gentiles for His name's sake" (Rom. 1:5). In other words, *not* preaching the gospel was not an option; not preaching the gospel equaled disobedience against God. This conviction was so strong that Paul believed he would be denounced by God for neglect of this: "woe is me if I do not preach the gospel" (1 Cor. 9:16). He rightly believed that, ultimately, his obedience in preaching the gospel would result in sinners being brought to the obedience of the faith—that is, a life of submission to the body of truth revealed by Christ in the Scriptures (Acts 6:7; 14:22; Gal. 1:23; Jude 3).

AUTHORITY IS ESSENTIAL BECAUSE OF THE DEVIL

Second, the work of making disciples of Christ is a frontal attack against the kingdom of the devil. Therefore, the unrelenting strategy of Satan to oppose the ministry of personal discipleship also accentuates our need for spiritual authority to build an army of soldiers for Jesus Christ.

The Bible refers to all unbelievers as children of the devil (1 John 3:10), born into his family because of the guilty, rebellious nature inherited from Adam (Rom. 5:12). Salvation is nothing short of a divine rescue mission whereby sinners are plucked out of the devil's grasping claws and graciously placed into the family of God and the kingdom of His beloved Son, in whom we are accepted (1 John 3:2; Col. 1:13; Rom. 15:7). David Doran summarizes it well in *For the Sake of His Name*:

> God's Word declares that Jesus the Lord has defeated Satan and his wicked host (Col 2:15) and that the Lord will soon crush Satan under the feet of the church (Rom 16:20). However, while the church waits for the final defeat of Satan it must remember that the task of making disciples calls it to raid his kingdom of darkness to deliver the god of this world's captives (cf. 2 Cor 4:4; 2 Tim 2:26). It would be foolish to think that the church can do this on the basis of its own authority. The church must engage in this conflict on the solid ground of the authority of the Lord of lords and King of kings.[12]

We now possess this same authority. When Jesus boldly declared, "I will build My church," He also promised that "the gates of Hades will not overpower it" (Matt. 16:18). Therefore, we can carry out the work of discipleship with the same confidence.

The God of salvation has not given us a mission that is dependent on human resources. Rather, the Great Command is accompanied by the authority to carry it out. To obey our risen Lord in this assignment, we must keep the obedience of the gospel before the minds of those we are discipling, knowing that we wage war against the forces of evil. Thanks be to God that the resurrected Jesus has rendered the devil powerless, and that His delegated authority will grant us the victory (Heb. 2:14; 1 Cor. 15:57).

Actions of disciple-makers

The Great Command also prescribes the actions necessary to produce lifelong followers of Jesus Christ. Three actions form the basic ingredients of the disciple-making process: evangelizing, baptizing, and teaching (Matt. 28:19–20a).

EVANGELIZING: WE MUST TELL OTHERS TO REPENT AND BELIEVE

First, the authority of Jesus Christ is to be employed to evangelize "all the nations." "Go therefore" is the translation of a participle meaning "in your going," which clearly implies continual responsibility to take the initiative in using our delegated power to make worldwide discipleship a reality. Having embraced the gospel as a command, we need to realize that God has made us responsible for telling others of Jesus Christ because He has ordained that saving faith only be birthed through the vehicle of gospel preaching (Rom. 10:14–17).

The message that Jesus preached is "repent and believe in the gospel" (Mark 1:15), and Luke's restating of the Great Command includes this important phrase: "that repentance for forgiveness of sins would be proclaimed in His name to all the nations" (Luke 24:47). Repentance is the flipside of faith; they go together as two sides of the same coin, "Siamese twins,"[13] or "inseparable graces,"[14]—two concepts that must not be divorced. In other words, the saving faith of the Bible is a repentant faith. There is no turning to God without a turning away from sin. Repentance is essentially a change of mind but, like faith, it involves the heart of man in its entirety: intellect, emotion, and will. The word "repentance" comes from the Greek word *metanoia*: *meta* meaning "after," or "change," and *noia*, "to perceive." Literally, it means "to change one's mind or purpose ... always, in the New Testament, involving a change for the better. The subject chiefly has reference to 'repentance' from sin."[15] Wayne Grudem defines repentance as "a heartfelt sorrow for sin, a renouncing of it, and a sincere commitment to forsake it and walk in obedience to Christ."[16] Clearly, biblical repentance is more than sorrow or regret over failing to meet God's standard (2 Cor. 7:9); rather, it includes a decision to turn from sin toward a life of righteousness.

Like faith, repentance is not a work of man, but a gift from a merciful God (Eph. 2:9; Acts 5:31; 11:18; Rom. 2:4). According to the teaching of Paul, pastor-elders need to be able to gently correct those in errant doctrine so that "perhaps God may *grant them repentance* leading to the knowledge of the truth" (2 Tim. 2:25). Repentance is not the product of human effort, but the gracious work of the Holy Spirit preparing sinners to approach a holy God on His terms rather than their own. Neglecting the preaching of repentance downplays sin, which in turn cheapens the message of the cross, undermining the progress of the gospel. It is critical that we not view repentant faith as merely a one-time event in the life of a disciple, but rather as a constant necessity and a work of the Holy Spirit, bringing us to an ever-deepening awareness of the depth of our depravity and also firming up our faith-grip on the Savior.

BAPTIZING: WE MUST TEACH OTHERS TO IDENTIFY WITH CHRIST

Second, we must teach water baptism as a condition of discipleship—the first command of Christ to be obeyed. If would-be followers of Jesus are not willing to obey this simple command, the likelihood of further obedience is questionable. Baptism is clearly presented as a command in the New Testament, as evidenced in five ways: First, Jesus commands baptism in the main text under consideration in this chapter (Matt. 28:18–20). He also approved of and exemplified obedience to baptism when He humbly submitted to being publicly immersed in the river by John the Baptist, which pleased the Father (Luke 3:21–22). Second, Peter commands obedience to baptism. Acts 10:46–48 says, "Then Peter answered, 'Surely no one can refuse the water for these to be baptized who have received the Holy Spirit just as we did, can he?' And *he ordered them* to be baptized in the name of Jesus Christ." Third, Philip administered baptism after the Holy Spirit led him on a short-term evangelistic mission that resulted in the fruit of conversion for an Ethiopian eunuch returning home from Jerusalem (Acts 8:26–39). When Philip's divine commission of leading this new believer through the obedience of baptism was complete, the Spirit snatched him away to another preaching assignment. Fourth, baptism was the expected response of believers in Christ in the New Testament church (Acts 2:38, 41;

8:12–13, 36, 38; 9:18; 10:47–48; 16:15, 33; 18:8; 19:5). Fifth, Paul assumes the obedience of baptism in his teaching by using it as a picture of how deeply the believer has been immersed in union with Christ, "having been buried with Him in baptism, in which you were also raised up with Him through faith in the working of God, who raised Him from the dead" (Col. 2:12). "Or do you not know that all of us who have been baptized into Christ Jesus have been baptized into His death?" (Rom. 6:3). Baptism is given as a command to the church and is, therefore, a demonstration of commitment to discipleship, which is central to the life and ministry of the local church.

Ligon Duncan and Susan Hunt make the same observation in their book *Women's Ministry in the Local Church*:

> The Church is the essential vehicle of evangelism and discipleship and the defender of the faith. The privilege of preserving and propagating the gospel was entrusted to the church by Jesus when He said, "All authority in heaven and on earth has been given to me. Go therefore and make disciples of all nations, baptizing them …" (Matthew 28:18–19). One of the things this means is that discipleship is to take place in the local church because that is where you baptize. The local congregation is where the truth is communicated to the next generation. The local church is where God especially meets with His people in the new-covenant era, and it is the essential instrument through which He propagates the truth.[17]

Since the local church is the focus of God's work in this age, and making disciples is our primary occupation, we must be faithful to teach others the importance of baptism. The Bible makes it clear that this is an essential part of leading others to live in obedience to the Lordship of Christ.

Teaching: We must train others to obey Christ

Third, making disciples of Jesus includes "teaching them to observe" all that Jesus commanded (Matt. 28:20). The teaching that Jesus had in mind was to be "a continuous process, not subordinate to and preparing for baptism, but continuing after baptism with a view to enabling disciples to walk worthily of their vocation … The teaching is with a view not to *gnosis* [knowledge] but to practice; the aim not orthodox opinion but right living."[18] Paul echoes this principle when he entreats the believers in Ephesus "to walk in a manner worthy of the calling with which you have been called" (Eph. 4:1).

Jesus' emphasis on doing His Word is clear. The word translated "observe" means "to guard, keep,"[19] and "to give heed to," as in "keeping commandments."[20] In other words, Jesus was not content to have followers who observed His teachings merely for religious admiration, but He insisted that they *act* upon them. The Great Command is not to make disciples who merely profess faith in Christ, but those whose obedience to God's Word bears witness to their verbal confession. As disciple-makers, we must realize that if we are not training believers to pattern their lives after Jesus Christ as revealed in the written Word of God, then we are not making disciples, no matter how many "decisions for Christ" we may encourage or even witness. Therefore, the discipleship process must continue to move toward the goal of each follower of Jesus Christ consistently displaying a life-pattern that honors God by submitting to His authority through active submission to His Word.

Since biblical knowledge without application leads to pride and self-deception, we cannot neglect this crucial ministry of training believers to live biblically. The book of James warns of the deceptive power of inactive hearing:

> But prove yourselves doers of the word, and not merely hearers who delude themselves. For if anyone is a hearer of the word and not a doer, he is like a man who looks at his natural face in a mirror; for once he has looked at himself and gone away, he has immediately forgotten what kind of person he was. But one who looks intently at the perfect law, the law of liberty, and abides by it, not having become a forgetful hearer but an effectual doer, this man will be blessed in what he does.
>
> James 1:22–25

The point is quite simple: God blesses humble, heart obedience to His Word because He equates it with obedience to Himself. Iain Murray is correct when he concludes, "Faithfulness to God and faithfulness to Christ are synonymous with faithfulness to their words."[21] The testimonies of both Jesus and the apostles establish this foundational principle.

Testimony of Jesus
- "For whoever does the will of My Father who is in heaven, he is My brother and sister and mother" (Matt. 12:50).
- "So Jesus was saying to those Jews who had believed Him, 'If you

continue in My word, then you are truly disciples of Mine; and you will know the truth, and the truth will make you free'" (John 8:31–32).

- "My sheep hear My voice, and I know them, and they follow Me" (John 10:27).
- "If you love Me, you will keep My commandments" (John 14:15).
- "He who has my commandments and keeps them is the one who loves Me; and he who loves Me will be loved by My Father, and I will love him and will disclose Myself to him" (John 14:21).
- "You are My friends if you do what I command you" (John 15:14).
- "Everyone who is of the truth hears My voice" (John 18:37).

Testimony of the apostles
- "But thanks be to God that though you were slaves of sin, you became obedient from the heart to that form of teaching to which you were committed" (Rom. 6:17).
- "Finally then, brethren, we request and exhort you in the Lord Jesus, that as you received from us instruction as to how you ought to walk and please God (just as you actually do walk), that you excel still more. For you know what commandments we gave you by the authority of the Lord Jesus" (1 Thes. 4:1–2).
- "By this we know that we have come to know Him, if we keep His commandments. The one who says, 'I have come to know Him,' and does not keep His commandments, is a liar, and the truth is not in him" (1 John 2:3–4).
- "The one who keeps His commandments abides in Him, and He in him" (1 John 3:24).
- "By this we know that we love the children of God, when we love God and observe His commandments. For this is the love of God, that we keep His commandments; and His commandments are not burdensome" (1 John 5:2–3).

The teachings of Jesus and the apostles are consistent: obedience to the Word of God is the hallmark of genuine saving faith. In other words, the chief mark of discipleship is a life that bears fruit for the glory of God by living in submission to the Lord Jesus Christ (John 15:8). This is not to say, however, that every disciple is obedient in every area of life—we are all in process—but it does contend that there is no genuine salvation without the fruit of obedience. Robert Coleman rightly concludes,

> If we have learned even the most elemental truth of discipleship, we must know that we are called to be servants of our Lord and to obey His Word. It is not our duty to reason why He speaks as He does, but only to carry out His orders. Unless there is this dedication to all that we know He wants us to do now, however immature our understanding may be, it is doubtful if we will ever progress further in His life and mission. There is no place in the Kingdom for a slacker, for such an attitude not only precludes any growth in grace and knowledge, but also destroys usefulness on the world battlefield of evangelism.[22]

We have not made disciples of Jesus Christ, and, therefore, have not obeyed the Great Command, until and unless we have taught them and are training them to walk in daily obedience to the commands of their new Lord.

This call to train others to obey the Word of Christ came as no surprise to the apostles, for they had listened to Jesus as He taught the principle of obedience. Earlier in the Gospel of Matthew, we find one of the clearest illustrations, most commonly known as the story of the man who built his house on a rock (7:24–29).

The main point of this story is hard to miss. It includes two men who are likened to two house builders. In that way they are similar. They are also similar in that both heard the words of Christ. However, the difference comes in their response to biblical teaching. The first man is wise, because he not only heard the words of Christ, but he also acted upon them. The second man is foolish, because he heard the same teaching, but did not apply it to his life. When the storms of life blew, the wise man's house (we could say his "life") endured because he built on the firm foundation of rock, while the foolish man's sandy foundation washed away with the tide.

Every time I teach this passage, I ask, "What is 'the rock' in this story?" Always, at least one person says, "Christ." But that is not correct. It is *obedience to the words of Christ.* Jesus said this Himself: "Everyone who hears these words of Mine and does not act on them, will be like a foolish man who built his house on the sand" (v. 26). Obedience to God's Word is the rock-solid foundation for the life of a Christlike disciple. In other words, we cannot separate disciple-making from the teaching of active, progressive obedience to the Word of God. Near the conclusion of his book *An All-Round Ministry*, Charles Spurgeon writes,

> [L]et us see to it that we set forth our Lord Jesus Christ as *the infallible Teacher*, through His inspired Word. I do not understand that loyalty to Christ which is accompanied by indifference to His words. How can we reverence His person, if His own words and those of His apostles are treated with disrespect? Unless we receive Christ's words, we cannot receive Christ; and unless we receive His apostles' words, we do not receive Christ; for John saith, "He that knoweth God heareth us; he that is not of God heareth not us. Hereby know we the spirit of truth, and the spirit of error." We must love and reverence all the teaching of our Lord; and we build our houses on the sand if we do not.[23]

Our attitude toward the Word of God reveals our attitude toward God Himself. To be indifferent toward the revelation of Christ in the Bible is to release oneself from an absolute, objective authority, which in turn undermines the biblical foundation of discipleship.

When we apply Jesus' story of the two builders to the task of disciple-making, we realize that, since both men heard the words of Jesus, but only one acted upon them, teaching the Word publicly is essential and critical, but it is not enough. We must come alongside fellow believers and help them to apply the words of Christ to their daily practice so that their lives are built on a solid foundation that will stand the test of any and every storm that God's providence may send their way. This demands the intensely focused, personal form of targeted discipleship that we call *counseling*. In other words, we must guard and work against the severance of daily living from Bible knowledge, which has become too common in today's form of Christianity.

Jesus used the authority from His Father to call followers to a life of uncompromising obedience to His words. Matthew records, "When Jesus had finished these words, the crowds were amazed at His teaching; for He was teaching them as one having authority, and not as their scribes" (7:28–29). This same authority is now ours to do the very same thing—to carry on His unfinished work of making disciples by evangelizing, baptizing, and teaching them to make steady progress in learning to obey His Word.

Assurance to disciple-makers

How shall we undertake such an enormous task? We must trust the promise of Jesus to work side by side with us as we carry out the Great Command: "and lo, I am with you always" (Matt. 28:20b). This promise was undoubtedly a reference to the indwelling ministry of the Holy Spirit who would teach the disciples all things and bring to their remembrance all that Jesus had instructed (John 14:26). Jesus promised that the Spirit would bear witness of Himself through His disciples (John 15:26); and this same Spirit of truth would be not only with them, but actually in them (John 14:17). The presence of the Spirit, therefore, is the empowerment of the church to make disciples.

Jesus repeated this promise immediately before His ascension to heaven when He instructed the disciples to wait for the Spirit. Acts 1:8 records His words: "but you will receive power when the Holy Spirit has come upon you." The word translated "power" comes from *dunamis*. It is also translated "ability" or "might," and refers to the inherent ability to do or perform anything. In the context, Jesus was teaching that the natural power of the Holy Spirit, which is unnatural to man, would indwell His disciples, thus causing them to reproduce worldwide. A. B. Bruce describes this heavenly power in *The Training of the Twelve*:

> All that the apostles were to gain from the mission of the Comforter— enlightenment of mind, enlargement of heart, sanctification of their faculties, and transformation of their characters, so as to make them whetted swords and polished shafts for subduing the world unto the truth; these, or the effect of these combined, constituted the power for which Jesus directed the eleven to wait.[24]

Biblical discipleship is impossible apart from the constant working of the Holy Spirit in the hearts and minds of both counselors and counselees. The Spirit knows the mind of God, and He alone has the wisdom to know the human heart and what He needs to change in it as the disciple's will submits to the authority of Jesus presented in His Word—the mind of Christ (1 Cor. 2:10–16).

The Son of God promised His presence with His disciples, and, therefore, us, "to the end of the age" (v. 20*b*). Until Jesus returns and His work is complete, we can be assured of the continual presence of the Holy Spirit of God empowering us to use the authority of God's Word and His gospel to make followers of Jesus Christ. This habitual, enduring presence of the Spirit will carry out the Great Command through us as we obey. God's promise is sure: "I will never desert you, nor will I ever forsake you" (Heb. 13:5).

Summary

People come to faith in Christ at different ages, in various stages of life, and from diverse backgrounds. As we evangelize our world with the gospel, we soon discover that new disciples bring into the community of the faith all kinds of baggage from their past and even their present. Effective ministry, therefore, will require physicians of the soul, loving counselors, to help disciples overcome sin by coming alongside them to patiently train them to apply the Word of God to their own hearts. As a result, new thoughts and motives will produce new habits that glorify the righteous God of their salvation. This is what the life of the church is all about.

My heart resonates with the passionate vision of Steve Viars, pastor of Faith Baptist Church in Lafayette, Indiana. When being interviewed about his church's counseling ministry, he said, "Call it counseling; call it specialized discipleship. It doesn't matter. We want to be a progressive-sanctification machine, a discipleship factory. We want people changing and growing where God's Word and Spirit make each of us more like Jesus Christ through careful attention to the inner man. That is what brings honor to God."[25]

A commitment to discipleship means that we must not merely lead lost sheep back to God through evangelism, but that we must also shepherd and train them to consistently live out the truths of the gospel. Viars' use of the terms "machine" and "factory" in no way implies that biblical discipleship is mechanical or that it can be mass-produced. Instead, it is an individual, intensely personal, and ongoing process. This is authentic biblical counseling! This is God's will for His church!

The Great Command to us is to use every divine provision to make disciples of Jesus Christ who never stop growing on the lifelong journey of learning to obey Him through the sanctifying work of the Holy Spirit. Therefore, biblical counseling is not an option. It should not be something that some churches do while others do not. It is a universal mandate to all biblical churches committed to carrying out the work of Jesus Christ—to produce obedient Christ-followers by coming alongside people to bring them to Jesus and to help them grow in the personal application of the faith to their lives. In turn, they too will be spiritually reproductive, and the stimulating process will continue until Jesus returns at the end of the age. However, for the ministry of discipleship to begin, the Holy Spirit must first convert the sinner by His divine power. This supernatural work of God's sovereign grace is the subject of the next chapter.

For further thought and small-group discussion

1. Read Luke 6:40. Discuss the meaning of the terms "disciple" and "discipleship." Why is a proper understanding of these terms significant to the personal ministry of counseling?

2. Read 2 Thessalonians 1:7–8; 1 Peter 4:17; and 1 John 3:23. Discuss the importance of understanding the gospel as a *command* from God. What changes do you need to make to the manner in which you communicate the gospel to others?

3. Read Romans 10:14–17. Discuss the necessity of a clear understanding of the gospel to evangelism. Discuss the importance of public witness of salvation, both verbal, by confession, and visual, by baptism. Have you obeyed the Lord in both of these areas?

4. Read 2 Corinthians 7:9–10. Discuss the difference between biblical repentance and worldly sorrow. How does this affect the personal ministry of counseling?

5. Read John 14:15–28. Discuss the role of the Holy Spirit in the fulfillment of the Great Command to make disciples of Jesus Christ.

The conversion of depraved sinners

Chapter 3

Or do you not know that the unrighteous will not inherit the kingdom of God? Do not be deceived; neither fornicators, nor idolaters, nor adulterers, nor effeminate, nor homosexuals, nor thieves, nor the covetous, nor drunkards, nor revilers, nor swindlers, will inherit the kingdom of God. And such were some of you; but you were washed, but you were sanctified, but you were justified in the name of the Lord Jesus Christ and in the Spirit of our God.

–1 Cor. 6:9–11

Authentic biblical counseling stands in awe of the power of God's gospel to convert thoroughly sinful men and women from thoroughly sinful thoughts, actions, motives, emotions, and desires to Spirit-generated new creations that reflect the beautiful love and holiness of Jesus Christ—the Lord we are now called to follow. God's vision of discipleship, therefore, requires a theological understanding of the nature and effects of sin and of the work of His sovereign grace; not merely to reform sinners, but to regenerate, redeem, rescue, and thoroughly recreate them by reclaiming them for His own possession. Therefore, we must be convinced that, in order for a natural-born rebel who is against God's divine sovereignty to come to the place of voluntarily submitting his or her will to the authority of the Lord Jesus Christ and, as a disciple, obeying His commands, a supernatural revolution must take place in the inner person. Nothing short of an extraordinary work of God via the wonder-working power of the gospel message is required—a work called *conversion*.

Conversion is the child produced by the marriage of faith and repentance. One theologian defines it this way:

> *Conversion is our willing response to the gospel call, in which we sincerely repent of sins and place our trust in Christ for salvation.* The word conversion itself means "turning"—here it represents a spiritual turn, a turning from sin to Christ. The turning from sin is called repentance, and the turning to Christ is called faith. We can look at each of these elements of conversion, and in one sense it does not matter which one we discuss first, for neither one can occur

without the other, and they must occur together when true conversion takes place.[1]

Robert Duncan Culver, in *Systematic Theology*, writes, "When the contesting football teams change ends of the field and goalposts—a complete reversal of direction—it is called a conversion. This is strictly consonant with biblical and theological usage … The idea of a spiritual–moral reversal of direction—conversion—is endemic in the Bible from the LORD's appeal to Cain (Gen. 4:7)."[2] In other words, conversion is clearly evidenced throughout the Scriptures.

The numerous times when, in the Bible, sinners turned from sin to God demonstrate this. For example, "in their distress [Israel] *turned* to the Lord God of Israel, and they sought Him, and He let them find Him" (2 Chr. 15:4), and once the prophet Jonah finally decided to submit to God's command to preach the message of repentance, the citizens of Nineveh "*turned* from their wicked way" (Jonah 3:10). In Paul's testimony of his own conversion and call, he defends Jesus' command to bring the gospel to the Gentiles "to open their eyes so that they may *turn* from darkness to light and from the dominion of Satan to God" (Acts 26:18). He also thanks God for the Thessalonian believers who had "*turned* to God from idols to serve a living and true God" (1 Thes. 1:9). The word that Paul uses for "turned" is *epistrepho*, in the aorist tense, which indicates "an immediate and decisive change, consequent upon a deliberate choice; conversion is a voluntary act in response to the presentation of truth."[3] The apostle's choice of this word emphasizes the active part the Thessalonians had in their conversion.

While hardly a more passionate defender of God's sovereignty in salvation can be found, the Apostle Paul recognized that the outworking of God's election of sinners to salvation does not result in passivity on the part of the individual. This human activity in no way steals any ray of glory from the God of salvation because His regenerating grace makes it possible. Culver defends the Scriptures' recognition of both the human and divine aspects of conversion when he writes,

> [Sinners] both convert and are converted. It seems best to think of the divine
> act (or work) as regeneration and the human acts of repentance and faith as
> conversion … Conversion is no works-righteousness, meritorious, synergism
> of God and man. They move together but God initiates it by regenerating

the will or disposition ... God can and does penetrate our spirits by His spirit without destroying any faculty of volition, rather by setting it free to make right choices.4

In order to fully appreciate the necessity of conversion, we need to understand the depth of man's sinfulness and the nature of the human heart to live in rebellion against God's authority and to resist or replace His demand for singular worship.

Challenge to conversion

Man's rebellious nature is the great obstacle to conversion. The reason for this conclusion is better understood by uncovering a biblical definition of the nature of sin. Here are four characteristics of sin that underscore the necessity of a supernatural conversion.

WILLFUL INDEPENDENCE

Sin is willful independence from God. When God created Adam and Eve for His glory, He had intimate fellowship with them and provided that the enjoyment of this relationship would continue only within the sphere of obedience to His commands (Isa. 43:7; Gen. 2:7–25; 3:8–24). So when our first parents sinned, they chose to do the opposite of what had been commanded them; that is, they acted in willful independence of their Creator. Thomas Schreiner is correct when he writes, "sin is first and foremost a rejection of the supremacy of God and his lordship over our lives."5 Sin shows its defiant nature by actively resisting God's demand for obedience.

Isaiah 53:6 is a key verse to consider when defining sin because it emphasizes our sinfulness both by nature and by choice: "All of us like sheep have gone astray, each of us has turned to his own way; but the LORD has caused the iniquity of us all to fall on Him." Sin is universal in man; it has contaminated "all of us." Therefore, we have all wandered from God, but this wandering is not passive or faultless since we have also willfully "turned to [our] own way." This is why the Apostle John called sin "lawlessness," acting independently of law as if God had no authority over us (1 John 3:4). Thus Charles Horne wrote in his classic work, *The Doctrine of Salvation*, "Sin ... is not only a failure to obey the law of God and/or a violation of it;

it is also—and perhaps even more significantly—a deification of self and a dethronement of God."[6] Sin, in reality, is self-worship.

Selfish cruelty

Sin is not only willful independence from the Creator, but it is also utter self-centeredness. The human heart demands its own way and demands it *now*, regardless of the consequences its choices may bring on itself or on others. But it is not merely inconsiderate of others; sin also makes the sinner cruel. For example, once Adam and Eve dethroned God, it was not long before sin displayed its ugliness. Their firstborn son, Cain, envied his brother's righteousness and his acceptance with God and, in anger against God and man, first murdered Abel in his heart, and then carried out his desire by literally taking his brother's life (Gen. 4:4–8). This explains why the Apostle John used Cain's sin as a contrast to biblical love, which leads us not to hate others, but to lay down our lives sacrificially for their good (1 John 3:11–16). It also explains why Jesus exalted the two "love commandments" above all others when he answered the inquiring lawyer, "'You shall love the Lord your God with all your heart, and with all your soul, and with all your mind.' This is the great and foremost commandment. The second is like it, 'You shall love your neighbor as yourself.' On these two commandments depend the whole Law and the Prophets" (Matt. 22:37–40). There is a sense in which we may say that, if we would always love God and others perfectly, we would never sin. "Love does no wrong to a neighbor; therefore love is the fulfillment of the law" (Rom. 13:10).

Russian novelist Fyodor Dostoevsky realistically paints the depth of man's depravity in *The Brothers Karamazov*, the story of the murder of a despicable father by one of his four sons. While musing to his younger brother about the deeper questions of life, Ivan, the intellectual son, correctly observes the violent nature of man. "People talk sometimes of bestial cruelty, but that's a great injustice and insult to the beasts; a beast can never be so cruel as a man, so artistically cruel. The tiger only tears and gnaws, that's all he can do. He would never think of nailing people by the ears, even if he were able to do it."[7] The reason man's inhumane behavior remains more cruel than that of a wild animal tearing apart its victim is that an animal kills instinctively for survival, but man kills for self-exaltation, and since he is made in the image of God, his conscience condemns him.

The image of God stamped upon man sets him apart from the rest of creation and makes him morally accountable to his Creator. Being made in the image of God also establishes a permanent connection between man's actions toward man and man's actions toward God. In other words, an attack on man is an attack on God, his Creator. This is the theological underpinning of capital punishment. "Whoever sheds man's blood, by man his blood shall be shed, for in the image of God He made man" (Gen. 9:6). James built on this theology when he reasoned regarding the tongue, "With it we bless our Lord and Father, and with it we curse men, who have been made in the likeness of God" (James 3:9). Therefore, the effects of sin are not only spiritual, in the sense of impacting one's relationship with God, but they are relational on the human level as well. Sin disturbs human relationships and, as it does so, it disrupts the relation of the image-bearer with his Creator. When man's selfishness attacks other image-bearers, God is rightly offended.

TOTAL DEPRAVITY

Man's autonomous heart is enslaved to his depravity. When we say that man is *depraved*, we mean that he is continually under the influence of sin. And when we say that he is *totally depraved*, we mean that sin has negatively affected every aspect of man's being: intellect, emotions, and will, leaving him profoundly sinful at the very core of his being from the moment of conception. "Total depravity means that sin infects all of what a human is."[8] No part of man is left untainted. In other words, it is his nature to sin. Sin is what man does best.

Sin is more than a choice: it is also the powerful influence or magnetic pull behind the choice, which holds the sinner in voluntary bondage. Del Fehsenfeld, Jr. writes, "The problem with sin is first it thrills, but then it kills. It blinds and binds its victim."[9] Israel's King David understood this all too well when he confessed his adultery to God: "Behold, I was brought forth in iniquity, and in sin my mother conceived me. Behold, You desire truth in the innermost being" (Ps. 51:5–6). When the prophet Jeremiah confronted Judah's sin, he said, "The heart is more deceitful than all else and is desperately sick." But he went on to ask, "Who can understand it?" (Jer. 17:9). In other words, not only is man's heart corrupt, but also its corruption is accompanied by blindness to the depth of his own self-centeredness.

Chapter 3

Total depravity is sometimes called *total inability*,[10] since man's bondage to his corrupt nature has rendered him unable to do anything in his own power to remedy his extreme spiritual problem. Apart from Jesus Christ, man is helpless, dead in sin, and left alone to lustfully indulge the desires of his flesh and mind (Rom. 5:6; Eph. 2:1, 3). As a result, natural (unconverted) man does not understand the things of God and has no innate desire to know them (1 Cor. 2:14; Rom. 3:11). Only a God of grace and power can redeem such a person. In order for conversion to take place, the sinner must be quickened to spiritual life by *regeneration*.

Regeneration is the supernatural imparting of spiritual life to the sinner's heart by the Holy Spirit alone, resulting in a spiritually dead person being brought to life in Christ (Eph. 2:1; Rom. 3:10–18; 5:6; Col. 2:13). Though this operation takes place in an instant, regeneration results from the effectual call of God in what theologians refer to as the *ordo salutis*, the order of salvation. Before a spiritual corpse can be active in conversion by repenting and believing in the Lord Jesus Christ, the heart must first be made alive by the Spirit's call through the hearing of the gospel—the instrumental cause of faith: "So faith comes from hearing, and hearing by the word of Christ" (Rom. 10:17). Peter wrote of this, "for you *have been* born again not of seed which is perishable but imperishable, that is, through the living and abiding word of God" (1 Peter 1:23). In the same way, Jesus told Nicodemus, "Do not be amazed that I said to you, 'You must be born again.' The wind blows where it wishes and you hear the sound of it, but do not know where it comes from and where it is going; so is everyone who is *born of the Spirit*" (John 3:7–8). Man's spiritual unresponsiveness requires regeneration, and the dramatic result of this work of the Spirit is the turning of an enemy of God into a disciple of Christ: "And although you were formerly alienated and hostile in mind, engaged in evil deeds, yet He has now reconciled you in His fleshly body through death, in order to present you before Him holy and blameless and beyond reproach" (Col. 1:21–22).

Circumstances of conversion

A biblical illustration of conversion is seen in the body of believers that God redeemed in the thoroughly sinful city of Corinth. Noted for its immorality, the city contained the temple to Aphrodite, the goddess of fertility, which housed 1,000 temple prostitutes. Its reputation was so well known that to commit sexual immorality was to "corinthianize."[11] G. Campbell Morgan described Corinth as

> one of the greatest cities in the Roman empire, characterized by wealth, luxuriousness and lust, by extreme cleverness and the arguments of its philosophers. The language used then was supposed to be the highest form of the Greek language. There was a phrase of the time, "To speak as they do at Corinth," which meant they spoke with accuracy and beauty, and with artistic finish. Corinth was the centre of everything intellectual, on the level of their own philosophies; but it was rotten at heart, utterly corrupt, given over to every manner of lasciviousness.[12]

The good news is that God in His mercy chose to save some out of this corruption. As we study the apostle's description of the nature of their conversion (1 Cor. 6:9–11), we need to recognize that, previous to this point in the letter, Paul has already given a strong rebuke of their toleration of sin among professing Christians, particularly one "so-called brother" whose sinful lifestyle boldly contradicted his profession of faith (5:1–13).

Paul asks, "Do you not know?" (6:9). Of course they should have known. That was his point! It is a basic truth: "the unrighteous will not inherit the kingdom of God." Leon Morris notes that the word translated "unrighteous" "lacks the article in Greek, thus putting emphasis on the character of these people, not the unrighteous as a class."[13] Those who choose to remain in sin shall never inherit, "enter into full possession of," eternal life.[14] This is a solemn warning. Paul does not want them to be deceived or misled into thinking that a Christian can take grace for granted by living any way he or she pleases.

Counseling in light of conversion

The specific sins mentioned below merely serve as examples of some of the kinds of habitual sins that biblical counselors must help disciples of Christ to overcome. First Corinthians 6:9–11 is a critical passage to turn to when discipling people who have been converted from enslaving lifestyles.

FORNICATION

"Fornicators" (*pornos*) refers to those who practice "illicit sexual intercourse,"[15] but the term can be used of immoral people in general (Gal. 5:19). Paul warns against all sexual activity outside marriage. As followers of Christ, we live in a sensual society—yet that is not our root problem. Instead, Jesus exposes the human heart as the source of immorality: "from within, out of the heart of men, proceed the evil thoughts, fornications" (Mark 7:21). Our sensual age simply serves as a stimulus to trigger the lusts already resident in our hearts. As Joshua Harris reminds us, "Part of the challenge Christians face in a lust-filled world is remembering that neither sex nor sexuality is our enemy. Lust is our enemy and has hijacked sexuality. We need to keep reminding ourselves that our goal is to rescue our sexuality *from* lust so we can experience it the way God intended."[16] Our hearts are naturally bent toward fornication due to self-fulfilling lusts, but God's grace transforms us by implanting a new nature within us at the moment of conversion. "… He has granted to us His precious and magnificent promises, so that by them you may become *partakers of the divine nature*, having escaped the corruption that is in the world by lust" (2 Peter 1:4).

Targeted discipleship aims at helping the believer to understand his or her own resident passions and then to seek, by walking in the Spirit, to grow in wisdom, holiness, and self-control. Self-control will in turn help the believer to guard him- or herself from surrounding stimuli that will continue to act as lures toward immoral thoughts and actions.[17] Since the painful consequences of immorality will undoubtedly bring some unconverted counselees to us, discipleship counseling will also seek to evangelize them while we trust the gospel to powerfully rescue sinners and radically change them from the inside out.

A specific pattern of fornication that disciple-makers will continue to confront is our society's acceptance of cohabitation, that is, living together out of wedlock. If we as disciples of Christ are going to let our light shine in the midst of the darkness of immorality, we must, as Jeff Van Goethem says, "see cohabitation for what it truly is—a form of bondage that, in the end, robs people of God's best."[18] Compassion, therefore, will move us to speak the truth in love to unmarried couples who are content to "try marriage" apart from a God-honoring covenant. According to Scripture, Van Goethem concludes, "cohabiting relationships are placed in the category of sexual sin. They are not marriages. They are not trial marriages. They are not quasi marriages. Disguising them under terms like 'committed relationships' or 'domestic partnerships' doesn't change their status. We should not view them with ambiguity: cohabitation is sexual sin. These unions are unholy unions."[19] We must courageously counsel these couples with biblical teaching concerning the sanctity of the marriage bed so that they may repent of immorality and walk in holiness and truth.

ADULTERY

"Adulterers" differ from fornicators in that their immorality specifically violates a marriage covenant. When God officiated at the very first wedding ceremony, He declared, "they shall become one flesh" (Gen. 2:24). The reason why adultery remains so serious is because it brings a third party into the marriage bond—an intruder—thereby corrupting the one-flesh relationship and defiling God's sacred covenant. As Kent Hughes explains, "adultery and its kin are unique in their sacrilege and spiritual devastation. Adultery is a sin against the sacredness of *marriage*, the sacredness of *one's own body*, and the '*body of Christ*'—not just against the church, but against Christ Himself."[20] Since earthly marriage is a picture of Christ's relationship to His bride, the church (Eph. 5:32), the New Testament reinforces how jealously God guards it: "Marriage is to be held in honor among all, and the marriage bed is to be undefiled; for fornicators and adulterers God will judge" (Heb. 13:4). Not only is adultery an attack on marriage, but also, since marriage is the foundation of the family, the destruction caused by unfaithfulness is always far-reaching. Those ruined by adultery will agree with Proverbs 6:26: "For on account of a harlot one is reduced to a loaf of bread, and an adulteress hunts for the precious life."

A biblical philosophy of discipleship, therefore, must be prepared to teach couples how to practice biblical repentance and forgiveness, cultivate purity of mind, and rebuild marriages that have been damaged by unfaithfulness. But we must also intentionally work to strengthen every marriage in the church, because there is no such thing as a static marriage. Every marriage is either growing stronger or it is weakening.[21] Since marriage is the most foundational human relationship, the marriage and family-life passages of Scripture must be regularly taught from the pulpit and studied in small groups and one-to-one settings (Eph. 5:22–6:4; Col. 3:16–21; 1 Peter 3:1–7). Husbands need to be taught how to love their wives sacrificially and lead them unselfishly.[22] Wives also need to be encouraged and instructed regarding how to fulfill their God-ordained role in the home.[23] Parents need to be equipped to shepherd their children in the ways and knowledge of Christ.[24] The local church committed to the Great Command will find that proactive family discipleship will go a long way to strengthening existing relationships and equipping each member of the family for God-honoring living, which will become an effective outreach to a world shattered by sin.

Richard Baxter, a Puritan minister in the 1600s, is most readily recognized as the author of *The Reformed Pastor*. This publication was not entitled "reformed" for doctrinal reasons, but rather because it called for a *reformation* among fellow ministers of the gospel. It was corrective counsel in book form. Since its original appearance in 1656, *The Reformed Pastor* has been a sober call to ministers to be serious about the gospel and their own personal holiness. In his Preface written in 1829, William Brown states, "hard must be the heart of that minister, who can read it without being moved, melted, and overwhelmed, under a sense of his own shortcomings; hard must be his heart, if he be not roused to greater faithfulness, diligence, and activity in winning souls to Christ."[25]

However, there is another aspect of Baxter's pastoral ministry that is not as well known: that is, his devotion to family discipleship. He was convinced that one of the most important areas where the members of a local church need serious training is that of biblical family living, and his primary focus was on fathers:

> We must have a special eye upon families, to see that they are well ordered, and the duties of each relation performed. The life of religion, and the welfare and glory of both the Church and the State, depend much on family government and duty. If we suffer the neglect of this, we shall undo all. What are we like to do ourselves to the reforming of a congregation, if all the work be cast on us alone; and masters of families neglect that necessary duty of their own, by which they are bound to help us? If any good be begun by the ministry in any soul, a careless, prayerless, worldly family is like to stifle it, or very much hinder it; whereas, if you could but get the rulers of families to do their duty, to take up the work where you left it, and help it on, what abundance of good might be done! I beseech you, therefore, if you desire the reformation and welfare of your people, do all you can to promote family religion ... Get masters of families to do their duty, and they will not only spare you a great deal of labour, but will much further the success of your labours.[26]

It is my conviction that churches that will concentrate a good amount of their discipleship energy on the heads of households will not only perform

God's will, but will also end up cutting their "crisis counseling" load by a large percentage. This is not to say, of course, that well-ordered families are the solution to all our woes, but we would be exceedingly foolish to ignore the priority that God Himself has placed on them and their tremendous help to further the work of His church.

HOMOSEXUALITY

The next sin that Paul confronts is that of same-sex relationships, which he denounces with two terms. "Effeminate" literally means "soft" and refers to the passive partner in homosexual relations.[27] Simon Kistemaker says this word denotes "passivity and submission,"[28] and in Corinth probably referred to the male prostitutes who made themselves available for "worship" in the temple of Aphrodite. "Homosexual," however, refers to the active, recruiting partner.[29] Together, the terms describe same-sex behavior and undoubtedly condemn related sins such as cross-dressing, sex-change operations, and the blurring of gender roles so prevalent today.

The Scriptures unanimously condemn homosexuality as an abomination, a detestable thing to God, that defiles individuals and nations (Lev. 18:22,30). Rus Walton explains, "Sodomy promotes idolatry, invites false gods, and nurtures apostasies. It spawns additional perversions; it gnaws at the vitals and rots the soul—first, the souls of those who indulge in its lusts and evils and, ultimately, the soul of the nation which permits it to continue unchallenged."[30] God gave His law to protect His people from the destruction of sin and to expose the wickedness of man's heart, thus ushering in the hope, freedom, and forgiveness found only in His redemption. When homosexuality is redefined as a disease or genetic disorder instead of sin, hope is stolen from those who need it most, because it is not always God's will that we be healed of diseases, but it is always His desire that we be delivered from sin. Homosexuality is unnatural, being the result of one's rejection of the Creator and His natural order. The first chapter of Romans describes the degeneration of man, the downward spiral people naturally descend when they forget God; specifically, when they know God, but do not honor Him as such (Rom. 1:21–27). Rejection of God produces a darkened mind, which leads to idolatry. As a result, God pulls out all the stops and lets them become in their lives what they already lust for in their hearts: "for their women exchanged the natural function for that which is unnatural, and in the same way also the men abandoned the natural function of the woman and burned in their desire toward one another, men with men committing indecent acts and receiving in their own persons the due penalty of their error" (Rom. 1:26–27).

The good news is that, like other sin, homosexuality is forgivable, and homosexuals, like other sinners, are sought after by the Redeemer. The Bible brings hope to the homosexual by honestly naming his or her lust and behavior "sin," thus opening a door for the gospel. Jesus died for sinners in order to cleanse us, break us free from the grip of sin and make us right with God. He did not come to call the righteous, but sinners (Matt. 9:13).

Biblical counselors, therefore, must believe in the power of the gospel to truly deliver people from homosexuality so that we may lead them out of bondage into freedom in Christ. And churches that are serious about obeying the Great Command must reach out to homosexuals with the hope of the gospel. Ed Welch exhorts,

> Because of the love of Christ, the church should pursue homosexuals. And through its exaltation of Christ in preaching, corporate prayer, and worship, the church should attract homosexuals. It should minister the Word to those who are already in church by flushing out the self-deceived, exposing the dishonest, confronting the rebel, offering forgiveness to the guilt-ridden, and giving hope. The church should also welcome those who struggle with homosexuality but have never been part of the church. The church should surprise them with love, a sense of family, and the absence of self-righteous judgment. It should offer truth in a way that is convicting, attractive, and radically different from anything else the homosexual has ever heard.[31]

We must also realize that the struggle to overcome these temptations may ensue for a long time, as it did in Corinth. Targeted discipleship will not only seek to reach sinners but, once they are converted to Christ, it will also teach them how to live out their new walk of holiness and equip them to war against indwelling sin. By calling sin "sin," we offer the hope of deliverance to unbelievers and we assure Christians who have been delivered, but remain tempted, that God's grace will continue to empower them for lives of obedience as they daily submit to the Word of God. "Now to Him who is able to keep you from stumbling, and to make you stand in the presence of His glory blameless with great joy, to the only God our Savior, through

Jesus Christ our Lord, be glory, majesty, dominion and authority, before all time and now and forever. Amen" (Jude 24–25).

IDOLATRY

The Greek word translated "idolater" literally refers to an image worshiper.[32] The Old Testament contains examples of God's wrath against idolatry (e.g. the book of Judges). In the New Testament, the Apostle John warned us to guard ourselves from idols (1 John 5:21) and taught that the lake of fire will be populated by idolaters: "But for the cowardly and unbelieving and abominable and murderers and immoral persons and sorcerers and idolaters and all liars, their part will be in the lake that burns with fire and brimstone, which is the second death" (Rev. 21:8). God desires, deserves, and demands our singular worship. Therefore, Thomas Schreiner correctly notes that all human sins "have their fountainhead in idolatry."[33] Consequently, we must acknowledge the predisposition of our hearts to value earthly things or the satisfaction of our own lusts above God Himself (1 John 2:15–16). We must learn to heed the warning, "my beloved, flee from idolatry" (1 Cor. 10:14).

As biblical counselors, we must constantly challenge ourselves and our disciples to examine what are often referred to as "functional gods"[34] or "idols of the heart,"[35] the hidden desires and motives that drive our thoughts, words, and actions. We must begin to see the deeper changes that God wants to make in the innermost being. We all need the Spirit of God to search our hearts for "anxious thoughts," and open our eyes to any "hurtful way," so that we may learn to walk in God's "everlasting way" (Ps. 139:23–24). We all need the Word of God to cut through our native blindness and expose self-serving motives hidden in the depths of our inner man (Heb. 4:12; James 4:1–3).

GREED

"Greed" summarizes the other terms Paul mentions, which all refer to the sinful accumulation of things. "Thieves" refers to those who appropriate what is not theirs by use of fraud and in secret, in contrast to "robbers," who do so by violence.[36] The word "swindlers" is actually an adjective that is translated "extortioners" in the King James Version. The noun form denotes "pillage, plundering, robbery … (akin to *arpazo*, 'to seize, carry off by force')."[37] Whether dishonest gain is accomplished quietly or through the use of physical force, God hates all forms of greed. God's commandment, "You shall not steal" (Exod. 20:15), covers them all.

The Greek word translated "covetous" refers to one desirous of having more.[38] *Synonyms of the New Testament* contrasts the root word *pleonexia* with *philarguria*, "love of money" or "avarice," by saying the latter refers to miserly behavior, whereas *pleonexia* means "the ever-increasing desire of the person who has forsaken God to fill himself with the lower objects of sense."[39] In other words, misers may act out their greed by refusing to spend what they already have, while covetous people incessantly crave the possessions of others, though both are motivated by the same lust for more.

Paul instructs the young pastor Timothy to continue to warn wealthy Christians to beware of the snare of riches and to fight off their seductive power through gracious giving:

> Instruct those who are rich in this present world not to be conceited or to fix their hope on the uncertainty of riches, but on God, who richly supplies us with all things to enjoy. Instruct them to do good, to be rich in good works, to be generous and ready to share, storing up for themselves the treasure of a good foundation for the future, so that they may take hold of that which is life indeed.
>
> 1 Tim. 6:17–19

Disciple-makers must help followers of Christ to forsake dishonest gain by teaching them to think backwards from their false actions to the strong desires that drive them. Then we can call them to repent and forsake the "lust of the flesh and the lust of the eyes" so that they "do not love the world nor the things in the world" more than they love God (1 John 2:15–16).

DRUNKENNESS

The Bible always puts "drunkenness" in the category of sin and provides multiple illustrations of the consequences of its selfishness. For example, Noah's drunkenness after the Flood brought shame to his family, as did Lot's, when his daughters used wine to induce him to sleep with them to carry on the family name (Gen. 9:21; 19:32–35). Alcohol dulls one's spiritual senses as well. Jesus warns, "Be on guard, so that your hearts will not be weighted down with dissipation and drunkenness and the worries of life, and that day will not come on you suddenly like a trap" (Luke 21:34). Strong drink also destroys relationships: "Wine is a mocker, strong drink a brawler, and whoever is intoxicated by it is not wise" (Prov. 20:1). Finally, drunkenness depletes one's resources: "For the heavy drinker and the glutton will come to poverty" (Prov. 23:21).

Biblical counselors must hold steadfastly to the conclusion that "alcoholism" (an unhelpful label) is a sinful lifestyle rather than a disease. Ed Welch writes, "Instead of explaining the overpowering urge for alcohol as a disease, the Bible talks about our motivations and desires, forces so powerful that they can take over our lives. The Bible says that we first choose our addictions, and only then do our addictions choose us."[40] Unfortunately, this view is not the reigning mindset among those in the self-help industry. Instead, an ever-growing list of "isms" is used to explain every imaginable sin-struggle in man. The "disease model" is everywhere, but is nowhere more present than in the area of alcohol abuse. This is due in great part to the influence of Alcoholics Anonymous and its founder, Bill Wilson. Welch summarizes,

> The disease model was first popularized by Bill Wilson, the founder of Alcoholics Anonymous (AA), in the 1930's. A devoted pragmatist, Wilson did not use the disease approach because it was well supported by research; he used it because he thought it helped men and women to be more open about their drinking problem. In other words, he was using a metaphor: drinking is *like* a disease. Over the past fifty years, however, the disease model has lost its metaphorical quality and it has been shortened to "drinking *is* a disease." The disappearance of this little word *like* has made all the difference.[41]

We must reject the disease model as inferior to the sin model, and most unhelpful, because it implies that the root problem in the drunkard is biological rather than spiritual, which severs all connection to the hope of deliverance by God through the gospel. Instead of settling for the lesser hope of being a lifelong "recovering alcoholic," the Bible enthusiastically offers the drunkard full deliverance from his or her sinful habit and a completely new life in Christ.

Verbal abuse

A "reviler" is one whose weapon of choice is the tongue. The words of a worthless man are "like scorching fire" (Prov. 16:27). Proverbs 19:1 says, "Better is a poor man who walks in his integrity than he who is perverse in speech and is a fool." The strongest New Testament warning against the destructive power of speech is found in the book of James:

> So also the tongue is a small part of the body, and yet it boasts of great things. Behold, how great a forest is set aflame by such a small fire! And the tongue is a fire, the very world of iniquity; the tongue is set among our members as that which defiles the entire body, and sets on fire the course of our life, and is set on fire by hell.
>
> James 3:5–6

Because the tongue is so difficult to control, addressing verbal sins will occupy a great deal of time in the disciple-making process.

Biblical counselors, therefore, must help others see that their words are only part of their problem. Jesus taught, "But the things that proceed out of the mouth come from the heart, and those defile the man" (Matt. 15:18). The tongue must be controlled, yes, but heart anger, hatred, and the arrogance behind much sarcasm must be exposed and repented of (Matt. 5:22). Pride, anger, and hatred must be put off and replaced by biblical love that esteems others as more valuable than ourselves (Eph. 4:29; Phil. 2:3).

Herein lies a tremendous opportunity for the disciple-maker to model growth in sanctification, since the answer to correcting verbal abuse is not to stop talking, but rather to learn how to submit our tongues to the authority of Christ so that we can "Be kind to one another, tender-hearted, forgiving each other, just as God in Christ also has forgiven [us]" (Eph. 4:32). We need to walk in the power of the Spirit so that we can train ourselves and others to speak the truth in love (Eph. 4:15). Paul David Tripp calls this "speaking redemptively":

> Speaking redemptively is all about choosing our words carefully. It is not just about the words we say but also about the words we have chosen not to say. Speaking redemptively is about being prepared to say the right thing at the right moment and exercising self-control. Speaking redemptively is refusing to let our talk be driven by passion and personal desire but communicating instead with God's purposes in view. It is exercising the faith needed to be part of what God is doing at that moment ... Speaking redemptively is not a superficial matter of choosing the right vocabulary, but a fundamental heart commitment to choose words that promote God's work in a particular situation ... We do not want to indulge the passions and desires of the sinful

nature. We do not want to provoke another to sin through our own conceit and envy. We do not want to bite and devour one another with words. Rather, we are committed to serve one another in love with our words.[42]

It is clear that the warning in 1 Corinthians 6:9–11 is very useful in biblical counseling. All who practice these sinful lifestyles will not "inherit the kingdom of God" (v. 10). Paul's point is that these sins will keep a person out of heaven because they are worthy of condemnation and therefore must be treated seriously and repented of as sin, not excused as "sickness."

Practical warning

Since all of the above-mentioned sins also appear in the apostle's list of lifestyles that warrant church discipline (1 Cor. 5:9–13), the disciple-maker will need discernment to know when other witnesses must be brought into the picture to strengthen the admonishment (Matt. 18:15–20). If loving confrontation is not received and repentance not exhibited, then we must conclude that the person is unconverted and treat him or her as an unbeliever. This means that the person is no longer welcome at Christian gatherings where he or she may be allowed to wear the mask of hypocrisy, and all "counseling" must now be in the form of an urgent call to repentance. The authors of *On the Level* write of this kind of love:

> Genuine love is not a matter of feeling; it is placing the same value the Lord places on his redeemed ones. Jesus declared: *"This is My commandment, that you love one another, just as I have loved you"* (John 15:12). If one highly values his brother, he will carefully follow the instruction to *"admonish one another"* (2 Thessalonians 3:15) so that a brother will have all the resources necessary to understand his sin and to see the consequences sinful behavior has on godly relationships. Sin breaks fellowship with other believers. If one is not willing to deny himself the personal benefit of another's fellowship because of that brother's sin, he does not demonstrate the true character of biblical love for that brother.[43]

Biblical love recognizes the threat that sin brings into the life of a believer and, therefore, cares enough to confront the one in peril with firm warning and a loving call to obedience.

Revelation 22:14–15 is one such warning passage to use: "Blessed are those who wash their robes, that they may have the right to the tree of life, and may enter by the gates into the city. Outside are the dogs and the sorcerers and the immoral persons and the murderers and the idolaters, and everyone who loves and practices lying." Loving calls to repentance may include such texts as Hebrews 3:15: "Today if you hear His voice, do not harden your hearts"; or Matthew 11:28–30: "Come to Me, all who are weary and heavy-laden, and I will give you rest. Take My yoke upon you, and learn from Me, for I am gentle and humble in heart, and you will find rest for your souls. For My yoke is easy and My burden is light."

The biblical counselor must warn the "so-called brother" (1 Cor. 5:11) that heaven will not be populated by those content to remain in bondage to sin (1 John 5:18). However, he must also hold out the hope found in the reality that heaven will be occupied by many sinners who were once trapped in these sins, but have now washed their robes in the blood of Jesus. "Such *were* some of you" (1 Cor. 6:11). Praise God! Heaven will be filled with former drunkards, former adulterers, ex-homosexuals, ex-swindlers—and many more sinners who know from personal experience what grace is: God's sovereign choice to bestow favor on undeserving sinners, creatures He made in His own image, but who rebelled against Him.

However, though it is true that God's grace is undeserving and thus cannot be earned, believers in Christ must be careful not to abuse grace by carelessly turning it into a license for sin. Paul addressed this tendency when he asked, "What shall we say then? Are we to continue in sin that grace may increase? May it never be!" (Rom. 6:1–2). Grace is not the freedom to live as we please, but rather divine incentive and empowerment for holiness. "For the grace of God has appeared, bringing salvation to all men, instructing us to deny ungodliness and worldly desires and to live sensibly, righteously and godly in the present age" (Titus 2:11–12).

Changes from conversion

Returning to the sixth chapter of First Corinthians, the words "Such *were* some of you" (v. 11) are a bold declaration of the power of the gospel to change lives and lifestyles. The next word, "but," highlights a strong contrast between what they were in the past and what they now are in Christ. This is conversion. This is a turning from sin to God. This is what God's transforming grace looks like. Gordon Fee writes,

For Paul there is to be the closest possible relationship between the experience of grace and one's behavior that evidences that experience of grace ... But those who concern themselves with grace without equal concern for behavior have missed Paul's own theological urgencies. It is precisely for these reasons that the warning texts in Paul must be taken with real seriousness. Security in Christ there is, to be sure, but it is a false security that would justify sinners who have never taken seriously "but such *were* some of you." That is to whitewash the sinner without regeneration or transformation; Paul simply would not understand such theology.44

Some of the believers in Corinth had been rescued from these kinds of sins. Some had been guilty in experience, but all of them possessed the depravity capable of such living. Commenting on this passage, John Calvin writes, "For we must hold this, that man's nature universally contains the seed of all evils, but that some vices prevail and discover themselves more in some than in others, according as the Lord brings out to view the depravity of the flesh by its fruits."45 Maintaining this mindset will help us to always minister grace to fellow sinners rather than display a harsh spirit even when God's Word calls for firm rebuke. Paul describes the transforming work of God in three ways.

God regenerates dead sinners and forgives

God breathes His life into sinners by the washing of regeneration. Some in Corinth were "washed." The aorist tense refers to a decisive action in the past. In other words, at the moment God brought spiritual life into these dead sinners, there was a complete washing. Titus 3:5–6 says, "He saved us, not on the basis of deeds which we have done in righteousness, but according to His mercy, by the *washing* of regeneration and renewing by the Holy Spirit, whom He poured out upon us richly through Jesus Christ our Savior." The Apostle John refers to Christ as the One who loves us and "released us from our sins by His blood" (Rev. 1:5). We must never disconnect forgiveness from the atoning work of Jesus or we lose the only biblical ground of grace. D. A. Carson reminds us that "forgiveness is never detached from the cross. In other words, forgiveness is never the product of love alone, still less of mawkish sentimentality. Forgiveness is possible only because there has been a real offense, and a real sacrifice to offset that offense."46 Forgiveness is free to us, but it was not free for God. It cost the life of His only Son: "In this is love, not that we loved God, but that He loved us and sent His Son to be the propitiation for our sins" (1 John 4:10).

Biblical forgiveness is the release of a debt. It is the removal of guilt accumulated before God. The conversion of some in Corinth was the beginning of a brand new life; their past was wiped away or cast "into the depths of the sea," as Micah prophesies (7:19). "Forgiveness is clearing the rubble of the past so that something fresh and fine may be built in its place."[47] That is exactly what God does when He saves a sinner and begins a lifelong process of remaking him or her as a new creature in Christ (2 Cor. 5:17).

GOD SETS SINNERS APART AS HIS OWN POSSESSION

Not only does God hurl a sinner's past into the ocean of His grace, but He also sanctifies the sinner for Himself. "Sanctified" (1 Cor. 6:11) comes from a Greek word that means "to make holy" or "consecrate."[48] It comes from the root *hagios*, the word for "holy." In other words, God calls sinners out of their sin and sets them apart for the purpose of reflecting His holiness in the world. God "saved us and called us with a holy calling" (2 Tim. 1:9).

Sanctification speaks not only of our immediate setting apart at the moment of conversion, but also of God's ongoing work of spiritual growth in our lives. Paul writes to the Thessalonians, "But we should always give thanks to God for you, brethren beloved by the Lord, because God has chosen you from the beginning for salvation through sanctification by the Spirit and faith in the truth" (2 Thes. 2:13). Sanctification, growth in holiness, is the expectation of the Spirit's work in a believer's life, "without which no one will see the Lord" (Heb. 12:14). Millard Erickson defines sanctification as "the continuing work of God in the life of the believer, making him or her actually holy," so that the saved sinner bears "an actual likeness to God."[49]

The believer's sanctification is threefold: sanctification is *positional*, in that it refers to God's calling apart a sinner to Himself (Gal. 1:6); it is *progressive*, in that it refers to the ongoing work of the Holy Spirit in the life of the believer, conforming him or her to the image of Christ (2 Cor. 3:18; Col. 3:10); and is *ultimate* (glorification), in that it refers to the day when the believer's standing and present state become one, being completely holy on that day in glory (1 John 3:2; 1 Thes. 5:23). Jim Berg reminds us of the indispensable role of the Holy Spirit in this ongoing work: "Change into Christlikeness ... is not something we do *to* ourselves. It is something that happens supernaturally through the agency of the Holy Spirit when we expose ourselves to God's Word and He reveals to us His glory."[50]

GOD DECLARES SINNERS RIGHTEOUS IN CHRIST

Not only does God regenerate and sanctify sinners, but He justifies them as well. Justification is the legal act whereby God declares the sinner righteous on the basis of empty-handed faith in the all-sufficient death and resurrection of His Son (Rom. 4:25; Phil.3:9). "Legal" is an important word in this definition because it emphasizes the fact that justification is not experiential. Instead, it is an announcement in the "courtroom of heaven." Justification is not the act whereby God *makes* us holy; that is sanctification, which is a process. In contrast, justification is a one-time event that forever changes the sinner's standing before God based on imputed righteousness alone.

Imputed righteousness is the perfect righteousness of Christ credited to our "spiritual account" as a gift of God's grace, received by faith, at the moment of conversion. A key verse is 2 Corinthians 5:21: "He made Him who knew no sin *to be* sin on our behalf, so that we might become the righteousness of God in Him." God the Father imputed our sin to Christ while He hung on the cross. Then the Father judged Jesus in our place as if He were the guilty one. When we believe in Christ and trust in His atoning work on our behalf, the perfect righteousness of God's Son is imputed to us in place of our sin. God then declares us righteous, treating us *as if* we had perfectly obeyed His law just as Jesus did. This is the wondrous exchange! As a result, "those who receive the abundance of grace and of the gift of righteousness will reign in life through the One, Jesus Christ" (Rom. 5:17), "through whom also we have obtained our introduction by faith into this grace in which we stand" (Rom. 5:2). This is all of faith, not by works: "by the works of the Law no flesh will be justified" (Rom. 3:20); "we maintain that a man is justified by faith apart from works of the Law" (Rom. 3:28); "knowing that a man is not justified by the works of the Law but through faith in Christ Jesus, even we have believed in Christ Jesus, so that we may be justified by faith in Christ and not by the works of the Law; since by the works of the Law no flesh will be justified" (Gal. 2:16). However, this justification is inseparably married to a living faith that produces works that glorify God (John 15:8; Eph. 2:10; the book of James).

Chapter 3

Summary

Regeneration, sanctification, and justification—together, these three works of God shout triumphantly of the power of the Holy Spirit in conversion. Charles Hodge says of the Corinthians, "they had been converted, or completely changed. They had put off the old man, and put on the new man. Their sins, considered as filth, had been washed away; considered as pollution, they had been purged or purified; considered as guilt, they had been covered with the righteousness of God."[51] As we make disciples of Jesus Christ, we must tell people the truth about how God views sin and, at the same time, hold out hope to those in bondage. For such *were* some of us.

When God saves a sinner, He does it completely. He does it by His grace and for His glory alone. The grace of God, delivered to the sinner by means of the gospel of God, is the power of God to transform abusers, homosexuals, drunkards, and every other kind of sinner. This is conversion, a work performed by the Spirit of God through the Word of God. Jeremiah Burroughs testifies, "A sinner who has lived a long time in such and such courses of sin and wickedness comes to the Word of God, and the heat of God's Word works upon him so as to melt his heart. And then the Spirit of God comes and takes the heart of this old sinner and puts it into the mold of the Word and makes him a vessel of honor."[52] Spirit-produced conversion then begins a journey of transformation into the image of Jesus Christ. This process requires personal discipline to apply the reality of the believer's new position in Christ to the ongoing pursuit of practical holiness, which the next chapter will address.

For further thought and small-group discussion

1. Read 1 Thessalonians 1:8–10. Compare and contrast the biblical understanding of "conversion" with the modern church's emphasis on "making a decision" for Christ.

2. Read 1 John 3:4. Discuss the four characteristics of the nature of sin given in this chapter of *Counsel One Another*. Discuss the consequent need for the supernatural conversion of the heart.

3. Read 1 Corinthians 6:9–11. Discuss the significance of the words "Such were some of you."

4. Read 1 Corinthians 5:9–13. Discuss the difference between a true believer and the person that Paul calls a "so-called brother." What is the believer's responsibility toward this latter person? Why?

5. Discuss your conversion story with others in your study group.

The call to disciplined godliness

Chapter 4

Therefore, prepare your minds for action, keep sober in spirit, fix your hope completely on the grace to be brought to you at the revelation of Jesus Christ. As obedient children, do not be conformed to the former lusts which were yours in your ignorance, but like the Holy One who called you, be holy yourselves also in all your behavior; because it is written, "You shall be holy, for I am holy."

–1 Peter 1:13–16

Authentic biblical counseling recognizes God's holy calling for the believer and the disciple's personal responsibility for self-discipline, by the power of the Holy Spirit, to live in a manner worthy of his or her high position as a new creature in Christ. God's vision of discipleship, moreover, requires recognition of the war that rages within the believer as indwelling sin fights to maintain the dominance it once enjoyed prior to conversion. Therefore, we must recognize that the transformation targeted discipleship aims to accomplish involves the renewing of the mind by the Word of truth, the repenting of inner desires by the Spirit's power, and the replacing of sinful habits by the practice of godliness. In a nutshell, a return to the apostolic pattern of maintaining a connection between sound doctrine and the discipline of godly living is indispensable to the ongoing process of sanctification.

However, the late James Montgomery Boice observed that Christians are lazy and unwilling to persevere on the hard road of godliness. Instead, we tend to look for the easy way out. As a result, spiritual growth is often lacking. Boice suggested three ways in which we try to avoid the struggle against sin.[1] First, we tend to seek out *formulas*, simple recipes for spiritual success. Slogans such as "Let go and let God" or "Just let Jesus take control" are attractive to our spiritual slothfulness. Second, we are prone to look for a *new experience*, a charismatic-type of "second work of grace" that immediately transforms us from being a defeated Christian to a victorious one. Third, total *avoidance* of the struggle against sin is a common response. All these have one thing in common: they are ways of seeking to find spiritual victory in the Christian life without the daily grind of discipline, but that will never happen. Scripture repeatedly links progress in godliness to the disciplined effort of the disciple:

- "… *discipline yourself* for the purpose of godliness" (1 Tim. 4:7).
- "Now for this very reason also, *applying all diligence*, in your faith supply moral excellence, and in your moral excellence, knowledge …" (2 Peter 1:5).
- "Therefore, brethren, *be all the more diligent* to make certain about His calling and choosing you" (2 Peter 1:10).
- [Jesus said] "*Strive* to enter through the narrow door; for many, I tell you, will seek to enter and will not be able" (Luke 13:24).
- "Now *flee* from youthful lusts and *pursue* righteousness, faith, love and peace …" (2 Tim. 2:22).
- "So then, my beloved, just as you have always obeyed, not as in my presence only, but now much more in my absence, *work out your salvation* with fear and trembling" (Phil. 2:12).

Instead of passive slogans, the Bible uses words like "discipline," "strive," "flee," and "pursue." In other words, the Christian life is a call to a disciplined warfare against sin—a struggle to resist temptation and simultaneously apply God's practical righteousness—a battle that will last until the day of the Lord Jesus, when "we will be like Him, because we will see Him just as He is" (1 John 3:2).

Unfortunately, many disciples of Christ do not appear to be winning this war. In his book *Set Apart: Calling a Worldly Church to a Godly Life*, Kent Hughes writes,

> Our own time and place require that we take stock of what is actually happening in our culture and in the church. The evidence is pretty clear that we do not understand either of these as well as we should. Among evangelicals, there is a great disconnect between (on the one hand) what Christians believe and assimilate from sermons and Christian sources and how (on the other hand) they actually live … The contemporary evangelical church *is not* lacking for moral and spiritual instruction. It *is* lacking in its ability to remain uncontaminated by the unchristian thinking and morality of contemporary culture.[2]

In other words, Christians have become worldly. A quick glance at evangelicalism confirms this and leads the observer to conclude that there is not much difference between the lifestyle of the world and that of many professing disciples. Hughes cites a number of examples in his book, including the following five:

There is little difference between the world's *pursuit of material riches* and that of the average Christian. Believers today seem to be chasing after temporal, earthly dreams just as much as unbelievers. While those who do not know Christ continue to speed down the racetrack of personal pleasure, believers are becoming increasingly hedonistic themselves.

Television-viewing habits of Christians differ little from those of the world, which has resulted in the descent of sexual morals. Hughes writes,

> In a 1997 report before the Senate Subcommittee on the Oversight of Government Management, anthropologist Dr. David Murray argued persuasively that "TV proselytizes sexuality," that the young of our culture are being socialized in their sexual behavior by the examples and values of television. Television presents sexuality in a manner that is not only pervasive, it is treated as an exotic imperative, ungovernable, lusty, smoldering, involving impossibly perfect sexual athletes who are nearly Olympian in their beauty and bodily enhancement. Further, it offers their behavior as normative, natural, expected, condoned, and even to be encouraged.[3]

Violence is rampant. According to a study published in 1992, "the average child watches eight thousand televised murders and a hundred thousand acts of violence before finishing *elementary school* (sixth grade). These numbers more than double by the time they graduate from high school."[4]

Standards of modesty in dress have virtually disappeared, thanks in large part to the fashion, body, and beauty industries. Hughes quotes his wife's dismay, as recorded in her book *Disciplines of a Godly Woman*:

> If you are blind or from another planet, you may conceivably have missed the fact that modesty has disappeared. It is dead and buried! If you don't think so, go shopping with a teenager. The fashion gurus have made sure that every item of clothing today's teen girl might need was designed to provoke thoughts that are other than virginal. It calls to mind the prophet Jeremiah's exclamation: "Are they ashamed of their loathsome conduct? No, they have no shame at all; they do not even know how to blush" (Jeremiah 6:15).[5]

Sadly, the dress of many teens in the typical church youth group is not much different from that which is promoted by the world.

How believers *spend the Lord's Day* is another example of the lack of distinction between believers and the world. What was once a day dedicated to worshiping God with other Christians has, for too many, simply become more free time for independent recreation.

In light of this blending of Christian and non-Christian lifestyles, there is a massive need for the work of personal discipleship to return to the example laid down by the apostles. What I am referring to is the discernable pattern in many New Testament books whereby disciple-makers spent considerable time laying a theological foundation so that their disciples would have doctrinal stability, but then immediately built on that foundation with the logical application of doctrine to life so that they also developed a faithful testimony. This conscious transition from thinking theologically to living godly is often signified by the word "therefore." Consider three examples.

First, we see this pattern in the book of Romans. The first eleven chapters thoroughly establish a doctrinal foundation, but then chapters 12 through 16 present the logical application of that same doctrine to the readers' lives. Chapter 12 begins, "Therefore I urge you, brethren, by the mercies of God, to present your bodies a living and holy sacrifice, acceptable to God." In other words, "In light of the eleven chapters of theology I have just taught you, live differently. This is the will of God for you!"

Second, the book of Ephesians follows the same pattern. The first three chapters are filled with theology, while the last three deal specifically with the application of that truth to life. Chapter 4 begins, "Therefore I, the prisoner of the Lord, implore you to *walk* in a manner worthy of the calling." Paul is pleading with them to do something with the doctrine they have learned.

Third, this pattern is found in the book of Colossians as well. The first two chapters teach doctrine, while chapters 3 and 4 focus on how to live out that biblical truth. "Therefore as you have received Christ Jesus the Lord, *so walk* in Him" (2:6). The rest of the book is a description of how to practice the Lordship of Christ in our everyday lives. This pattern indicates that the New Testament writers never entertained the notion that theology was something to be learned in the head without effecting change in one's behavior.

This same pattern is evident in Peter's first epistle. In the first five verses, believers are assured that we are chosen by the Father, sanctified by the Spirit, and redeemed by the blood of the Son of God (1 Peter 1:1–5). Then in the next seven verses (1:6–12), we learn how cherishing the great inheritance that is reserved for us in heaven equips us to respond to trials in a way that glorifies God and is proof of our faith, "being more precious than gold" (v. 7). Verse 13 then consciously moves toward the application of this doctrine to a life of obedience to the truth:

> Therefore, prepare your minds for action, keep sober in spirit, fix your hope completely on the grace to be brought to you at the revelation of Jesus Christ. As obedient children, do not be conformed to the former lusts which were yours in your ignorance, but like the Holy One who called you, be holy yourselves also in all your behavior; because it is written, "You shall be holy, for I am holy."

> vv. 13–16

Once again, the word "therefore" marks a conscious transition from doctrine to practice. Peter calls disciples to war against sin by living out their great salvation through discipline of mind, heart, and life. Biblical counselors must learn to follow this training pattern.

Discipline the thoughts of the mind (1 Peter 1:13)

In order to grow in Godliness, we must understand the importance of renewing our minds by the Word of God. We need to be mentally prepared, alert, and hopeful for the return of Jesus Christ.

BE PREPARED

Living godly in an ungodly world requires preparation for the spiritual battle that exists. Consequently, Peter urges his readers to "prepare your minds for action" (v. 13a). The word translated "prepare" means "to bind, to gather up"; some translations have "gird."[6] In Peter's day, the people of the East wore long, loose robes that they gathered up into a girdle or belt when preparing for physical activity. As Elijah "girded up his loins and outran Ahab" (1 Kings 18:46), so believers are to get ready to run the Christian race (1 Cor. 9:24). Peter was essentially saying, "Tie up your girdles. Get ready for action!" Today, we would say, "Roll up your sleeves. Get ready to work!"

Peter's appeal to his readers to be prepared is pertinent because believers are "aliens" (1:1). That is, we are not primarily citizens of earth, but are foreigners whom God has scattered around the world to accomplish His purpose. Like the Israelites at the time of the Exodus, we must be prepared: "Now you shall eat it in this manner: with your loins girded, your sandals on your feet, and your staff in your hand; and you shall eat it in haste—it is the Lord's Passover" (Exod. 12:11). In Peter's letter, this "preparation" was a reminder of how quickly the Israelites fled Egypt, but it was also an urgent call to always be ready to move since his readers were pilgrims, strangers, and aliens in a foreign land. We too must discipline ourselves to remember that our true citizenship is in heaven, "from which also we eagerly wait for a Savior, the Lord Jesus Christ; who will transform the body of our humble state into conformity with the body of His glory" (Phil. 3:20–21).

It is crucial to notice that Peter's call concerns the "mind." Spiritual readiness is the result of how we think. Near the end of the Apostle Paul's description of the armor of God, we read, "Stand firm therefore, having girded your loins with truth" (Eph. 6:14). As disciples, we are to be truth-saturated, truth-driven people. This means that the Word of God should fill our minds and govern the way we think so that our lifestyles please the Lord. Since our hearts are "more deceitful than all else" (Jer. 17:9), Scripture is the only objective test of the acceptability of our thoughts to God (Ps. 19:14).

BE ALERT

A second essential element of godliness is also directed at the mind (v. 13b). "Sober" is the word Peter chose to use, and it denotes self-control or clarity of mind.7 Kenneth Wuest said that the word means "to be calm and collected in spirit, to be temperate, dispassionate, circumspect. It speaks of the proper exercise of the mind, that state of mind in which the individual is self-controlled and is able to see things without the distortion caused by worry, fear, and their related attitudes."8 When people turn away from alcohol, they are described as becoming "sober" because their minds are no longer controlled by liquor. They are calm and collected, in full control. In the same way, the New Testament calls disciples to practice spiritual sobriety, for four reasons.

First, mental alertness prepares us to endure difficulty for the sake of the gospel. The Apostle Paul wrote to Timothy, "But you, be sober in all things, endure hardship, do the work of an evangelist, fulfill your ministry" (2 Tim. 4:5). Simply stated, we should be serious-minded about serving the Lord.

Second, growing in holiness also requires us to be ready for Jesus' return. The Apostle Paul taught the church at Thessalonica: "But you, brethren, are not in darkness, that the day would overtake you like a thief; for you are all sons of light and sons of day. We are not of night nor of darkness; so then let us not sleep as others do, but let us be alert and sober" (1 Thes. 5:4–6). Surely we would not want Jesus to return to find us drunk with the wine of worldly philosophy.

Third, spiritual alertness leads to a disciplined prayer life. Later in his letter, Peter warned his readers, "The end of all things is near; therefore, be of sound judgment and sober spirit for the purpose of prayer" (1 Peter 4:7). In Matthew 26:41, Jesus warned His disciples, who preferred sleep over prayer, "Keep watching and praying that you may not enter into temptation; the spirit is willing, but the flesh is weak." This verse reveals a link between the discipline of prayer and the progress of godliness in the Christian life.

Fourth, in striving to maintain spiritual alertness, followers of Christ must recognize that we have an enemy who is crafty and subtle. In fact, Peter compared Satan to a lion that crouches as he stalks his victim: "Be of sober spirit, be on the alert. Your adversary, the devil, prowls around like a roaring lion, seeking someone to devour" (1 Peter 5:8). Lucifer was once the most beautiful and powerful of all God's angelic creatures but, having been lifted up with pride, he was cast down from his lofty position (Ezek. 28:1–19; Isa. 14:12–15) and now works night and day to oppose the saving work of God. In relation to unbelievers, he blinds their minds so that they may not see the glory of Christ (2 Cor. 4:4), plucks the seed of truth from their hearts before it can germinate (Mark 4:15), ensnares them in false doctrine propagated by demons (1 Tim. 4:1; 2 Tim. 2:26), and energizes false teachers (2 Cor. 11:13–15). In relation to believers, he accuses us (Rev. 12:10), opposes our ministry (Acts 13:10; 1 Thes. 2:18), and tempts us to sin (1 Thes. 3:5). Consequently, the greatest defense against Satan's destructive work is a mind that is constantly being renewed by the Word of truth. Warren Wiersbe agrees: "The believer's mind ought to be so saturated with divine truth that it can determine the divine perspective on every question, issue, or decision. A renewed mind is a mind alert to the world's false philosophies and Satan's subtle strategy."9

BE HOPEFUL

The third essential part of disciplining the thoughts of the mind is that of fixing our "hope completely" on the fullness of "the grace to be brought" to us (v. 13*c*). This is a perfect hope that focuses our attention on Jesus and the promise of His full revelation at His coming. The phrase "grace to be brought" is originally in the present tense, which means it is a grace that is being brought to us, that is, grace that is coming and is now within our grasp. According to Titus 2:11–13, this empowering grace compels us to live godly while we look for His coming: "For the grace of God has appeared, bringing salvation to all men, instructing us to deny ungodliness and worldly desires and to live sensibly, righteously and godly in the present age, looking for the blessed hope and the appearing of the glory of our great God and Savior, Christ Jesus." Notice the past, present, and future grace mentioned in these verses. The past grace of God has already appeared and has brought salvation to mankind. Future grace will be fully revealed when the Lord Jesus returns. However, sandwiched between the past and the future, God also supplies present grace. This present grace is constantly "instructing us to deny ungodliness and worldly desires and to live sensibly, righteously and godly in the present age." In other words, biblical grace does not lead us toward licentiousness. Instead, it sanctifies. It leads away from sin and toward righteousness. This present grace is a foretaste of the consummation of our salvation, which will take place when Jesus returns. To be holy, we must renew our minds with this "blessed hope."

Merrill Unger defines hope as the "expectation of good ... a joyful and contented expectation of eternal salvation."[10] It is a confident expectation that is based on the truth of the gospel and the promises of God in Christ Jesus. He Himself "is our hope" (1 Tim. 1:1) and God the Father "has caused us to be born again to a living hope through the resurrection of Jesus Christ from the dead" (1 Peter 1:3). He raised Jesus "from the dead and gave Him glory, so that [our] faith and hope are in God" (1 Peter 1:21). And since we are "heirs according to the hope of eternal life" (Titus 3:7), we must, necessarily, gird our minds for action; "everyone who has this hope fixed on Him purifies himself, just as He is pure" (1 John 3:3). As followers of Christ who continue to pursue holiness, we can be confident of the final completion of our sanctification that will take place when we see Jesus face to face. "Beloved, now we are children of God, and it has not appeared as yet what we will be. We know that when He appears, we will be like Him, because we will see Him just as He is" (1 John 3:2).

A critical part of the sanctification process is putting off the old self and putting on the new, "which in the likeness of God has been created in righteousness and holiness of the truth" (Eph. 4:24). However, this transformation requires first being "renewed in the spirit of [the] mind" (Eph. 4:23). The Apostle Paul taught this same pattern in the book of Romans:

> Therefore I urge you, brethren, by the mercies of God, to present your bodies a living and holy sacrifice, acceptable to God, which is your spiritual service of worship. And do not be conformed to this world, but be transformed *by the renewing of your mind*, so that you may prove what the will of God is, that which is good and acceptable and perfect.
>
> Rom. 12:1–2

According to this passage, worldliness is primarily a mental disorder; that is, a misuse of the Christian mind. Instead of slothfully conforming our minds to think like the rest of the world, we as disciples of Christ must discipline ourselves to think God's thoughts according to His Word.

The passage above from Romans begins with an urgent request in light of the mercy of God in bringing the redemption of Jesus Christ to sinners who are worthy of the wrath of God. Paul pleads, "present your bodies." This passionate plea calls for the offering of the believer's body to God for the service of holiness. This request is logical, because God owns us. "Or do you not know that your body is a temple of the Holy Spirit who is in you, whom you have from God, and that you are not your own? For you have been bought with a price: therefore glorify God in your body" (1 Cor. 6:19–20). This bodily sacrifice, unlike the offerings of the Old Testament, is *living*. However, in order for this sacrifice to be pleasing to God, it must meet His holy standard, which is both negative and positive.

God's standard for His disciples is negative in that we must not be "conformed." The word "conform" comes from a verb which, in this context, means "to form or mold after something."[11] This word is traditionally translated in the passive voice in Romans 12:2: "be conformed." This passivity has been popularized by some translations, such as that of J. B. Phillips.[12] However, the Greek form also allows for the middle voice, which would read, "do not conform yourselves."[13] The middle voice places the responsibility for personal godliness where it belongs—on the shoulders of the disciples who are called to be holy. Consequently, this verse is not only telling us to beware of the world conforming us into its mold, but it also discourages us from patterning ourselves after the world by adopting its values, priorities, and attitudes. Since Jesus died to deliver us from the world, to follow its standards is not an acceptable response to God's call to holiness. According to Galatians 1:4, Jesus "gave Himself for our sins *so that He might rescue us from this present evil age*, according to the will of our God and Father."

God's standard for disciples is also positive: "be transformed." The Greek word translated "transformed' comes from the word from which we get "metamorphosis." John Stott notes that this word

> is the verb used by Matthew and Mark of the transfiguration of Jesus. And although the evangelists vary in saying that it was his skin, his face and his clothing which shone, Mark is clear that he himself "was transfigured before them." A complete change came over him. His whole body became translucent, whose significance the disciples would not be able to understand, Jesus implied, until after his resurrection. As for the change which takes place in the people of God, which is envisaged in Romans 12:2 and 2 Corinthians 3:18 (the only other verses in which μεταμορφόω occurs), it is a fundamental transformation of character and conduct, away from the standards of the world and into the image of Christ himself.[14]

This complete transformation into the image of Jesus is the work of the Holy Spirit: "But we all, with unveiled face, beholding as in a mirror the glory of the Lord, are being transformed into the same image from glory to glory, just as from the Lord, the Spirit" (2 Cor. 3:18). However, this work of the Spirit requires personal discipline on the part of the disciple, which begins with renewing the mind, "beholding as in a mirror the glory of the Lord."

The word translated "renewing" means to cause something "to be new and better."[15] That is, renewing the mind means washing out the worldly ways of thinking which inhabit the Adamic nature by filling it with a new, fresh supply of God's way of thinking as found in the Scriptures. The "mirror" in which we behold the Lord Jesus is the Word of God (see James

1:23). Ephesians 5:26 says that Christ sanctifies His church by means of "the washing of water with the word." It is the disciple's personal responsibility to meditate on the Word of God day and night (Ps. 1) and take "every thought captive to the obedience of Christ" (2 Cor. 10:5) so that what does not glorify Christ may be rejected. Philippians 4:8 provides a great litmus test for all our thoughts: "Finally, brethren, whatever is true, whatever is honorable, whatever is right, whatever is pure, whatever is lovely, whatever is of good repute, if there is any excellence and if anything worthy of praise, dwell [think, meditate] on these things." Biblical counselors will want to use this verse as a test in order to help their counselees learn to discern their thought patterns. For example, counselors may want to have those who are struggling with impure thoughts print the text of Philippians 4:8 in large letters, frame it, and set it on top of their televisions or computers so that God's standard becomes the guide for what is viewed. This is merely one example of the use of Scripture to confront existing thought patterns. This discipline of renewing the mind will lead to the promised reward—the full approval of the will of God, that which is "good and acceptable and perfect" (Rom. 12:2).

The author of Hebrews understood the power of meditating on Jesus Christ and His saving work. Instead of being mesmerized by the world's media, today's disciples are called to keep "fixing [their] eyes on Jesus, the author and perfecter of faith, who for the joy set before Him endured the cross" (Heb. 12:2). David Brainerd, missionary to the American Indians, wrote in his journal of how meditating on the gospel helps the pursuit of holiness:

> I never got away from Jesus and him crucified. When my people were gripped by this great evangelical doctrine of Christ and him crucified, I had no need to give them instructions about morality. I found that one followed as the sure and inevitable fruit of the other ... I find my Indians begin to put on the garments of holiness and their common life begins to be sanctified even in small matters when they are possessed by the doctrine of Christ and him crucified.[16]

Remembering the suffering and death that our Savior endured to free us from the power and penalty of sin urges us toward the discipline of godliness. If we fix our eyes on Him and the price He paid to redeem us, we will be more likely to discipline our thoughts to meditate on what pleases Him.

Discipline the lusts of the heart (1 Peter 1:14)

The call to godly discipline also requires a transformation of the inner motives of the heart. Peter continues, "As obedient children, do not be conformed to the former lusts which were yours in your ignorance." Our motive for living a godly life needs to be our love for and obedience to the One who saved us by His grace alone. We should be known as "obedient children" of God. In order to be like this, we are not to be conformed to our "former lusts," in other words, we must not live the way we did before our conversion. Wuest said that this conformity refers to "the believer masquerading in the costume of the world."[17] Instead of remaining driven by former lusts and fashioning ourselves like the unregenerate in the world, there is to be a clean break from the sins that characterized our former lifestyles (1 Peter 4:2–3). However, this exposes two significant problems of the human heart.

THE PROBLEM OF INSATIABLE LUSTS

Deep within the human heart lie major obstacles to the ongoing process of sanctification—the "former lusts" that Peter urged believers to deliberately lay aside. These strong desires are further exposed by James, the brother of our Lord:

> What is the source of quarrels and conflicts among you? Is not the source your pleasures that wage war in your members? You lust and do not have; so you commit murder. You are envious and cannot obtain; so you fight and quarrel. You do not have because you do not ask. You ask and do not receive, because you ask with wrong motives, so that you may spend it on your pleasures.
>
> James 4:1–3

The first recipients of these pointed words were Jewish believers who were "dispersed abroad" (1:1). MacArthur notes that this dispersion was possibly "a result of Stephen's martyrdom (Acts 7, AD 31–34), but more likely due to the persecution under Herod Agrippa I (Acts 12, ca. AD 44)."[18] However, a much deeper problem than the outward persecution these believers were experiencing concerned the self-centered desires that were causing conflicts among them. Subsequently, the Holy Spirit used James to pen words that would perform heart surgery on his readers by exposing their corrupt motives.

James answered his own question about the source of their habitual quarrels, describing it as being their "pleasures." The original Greek word is that from which we get our word "hedonism," which "denotes the enjoyment derived from the fulfillment of one's desires, or, as here, the craving for the pleasure itself ... the yearnings of self-love."[19] Earlier in his letter, James revealed the origin of sinful temptations as the enticement of our own lust (1:14). Scripture never allows us to shift the blame for our sin anywhere else. Our sin is *always* our responsibility. Unlike Moses, we often choose "the passing pleasures of sin" (Heb. 11:25) because that is exactly what our hearts crave.

These self-centered desires "wage war" in our bodily "members" (compare James 3:6). Harry Ironside defines these lusts as "unrestrained and unlawful desires struggling for fulfillment in our very being."[20] Hiebert identifies these passions as "conflicting cravings, which throw the individual into inner turmoil ... the expressions of the believer's old nature seeking self-satisfaction."[21] In other words, deep within the heart are self-loving desires that are so strong and so determined to be satisfied that, when thwarted, lead to conflicts with those who get in the way of their fulfillment. "You lust and do not have; so you commit murder. You are envious and cannot obtain; so you fight and quarrel" (4:2). These desires then often become idols of the heart which, if unrepented of, easily produce resentment and bitterness toward fellow brothers and sisters in Christ. Jerry Bridges identifies this self-love in *The Practice of Godliness*: "Resentment, bitterness, and self-pity build up inside our hearts and eat away at our spiritual lives like a slowly spreading cancer. All of these sinful inner emotions have in common a focus on self. They put our disappointments, our wounded pride, or our shattered dreams on the thrones of our hearts, where they become idols to us."[22]

"Idolatry" is not too strong a word to describe what frequently occurs in our hearts for, as the passage continues, James reveals our natural tendency to pursue the fulfillment of these pleasures independently of God—"You do not have because you do not ask." Hiebert says of those to whom James wrote, and, therefore, also of us, "Instead of turning to God as the Giver of every good and perfect gift (1:17), they attempt to satisfy their gnawing wants through their own efforts. Their approach is self-centered and worldly. Instead of wrestling with God in prayer, they wrangle bitterly with men."[23] Since not all desires are evil, it is legitimate for us to pray to God regarding them. However, good desires become evil when we satisfy them ourselves in a fleshly manner apart from seeking God's will. "You ask and do not receive, because you ask with wrong motives, so that you may spend it on your pleasures" (4:2–3).

Consequently, growing in holiness requires an increasing awareness of the hidden lusts of our hearts that motivate us to do what we do. As we become aware of these self-glorifying motives, we must repent of them and yield to the Spirit's ability to completely reform our desires and replace them with the all-consuming desire to please God. Like Paul, we need to make this our highest ambition: "whether at home or absent, to be pleasing to Him" (2 Cor. 5:9).

The task of biblical counselors is to help disciples look beneath their conflicts to identify the self-serving motives that seek preeminence within them. There will be no lasting growth in godliness if we fail to expose the sinful longings of the heart (what truly motivates us) and thus identify what it is we crave so badly that we are willing to displease God in order to get it. Once these self-centered desires are identified, we must repent of them and make pleasing God our chief pursuit. This inner conflict is the same one that the Apostle Paul expounded on in the book of Romans, which exposes the problem of indwelling sin.

The Problem of Indwelling Sin

To fully comprehend the challenge every disciple faces in the quest for godliness, a summary of the teaching of the sixth and seventh chapters of the book of Romans is in order. Here, the Apostle Paul provides a glimpse of his own battle against sin from which we can learn much about the reality of the struggle of discipleship.

Dead to sin, alive to God

Romans 6 presents the right way to win the battle against sin through the ongoing recognition that, by virtue of spiritual union with Christ, the believer in Jesus Christ is "dead" to sin and "alive" to God. Since we know these things to be true, we must embrace them by faith. "Even so consider yourselves to be dead to sin, but alive to God in Christ Jesus" (6:11).

The classic screenplay *Fiddler on the Roof* provides a fitting illustration.

The main character, Tevye, is a Jewish man living in Tsarist Russia. The heart of the film is Tevye's struggle to accept the cultural changes that are turning his world upside down, especially through the non-arranged marriages of three of his five daughters. We empathize with his internal pain as we watch "tradition," the glue that held his little world together, begin to dissolve before his very eyes. Tzeitel, the oldest daughter, is in love with Motel, the tailor, but no one knows except the two of them. So, when the matchmaker informs Tzeitel's parents that the village butcher, Lazar Wolf, is interested in their daughter, they get very excited. Though he is old and she is young, he is wealthy, so at least their daughter, who was raised in poverty, will never know hunger again. For this reason, Tevye makes a bargain with the butcher. Of course, when Tzeitel is informed of her parents' choice of a husband, she is horrified and begs and pleads with her father not to make her marry Lazar Wolf because she is really in love with Motel and, after all, they "gave each other a pledge." Reluctantly, not wanting to see his daughter miserable her whole life, Tevye breaks his agreement with the butcher and lets his daughter marry the timid tailor.

The second daughter's name is Hodel and her affections soon become attached to a young, outspoken man named Perchik. Perchik is motivated by a desire to preserve freedom through revolution and, as a result of his actions, is thrown into prison and shipped to Siberia. When he writes to request that Hodel come to him, she chooses to leave her family and travel across the frozen wasteland to join him in marriage.

By this time, Tevye has reluctantly begun to accept this new practice of a man and a woman choosing for themselves whom they should marry. But even Hodel's engagement could never have prepared him for his final daughter's choice. Chava is the youngest daughter in the story whose affections turn toward a fellow lover of books, Fyedka. However, there is a vast gulf between her choice and that of her older sisters. They married fellow Jews. Fyedka, however, is a Gentile, forbidden territory for a young Jewish girl. But her father's command to not marry outside the faith falls on stubborn ears and Chava and Fyedka elope. Tevye learns of it while walking in the field behind his plow. As Golde, his wife, runs toward him shouting, he asks what is wrong and she informs him of their youngest daughter's marriage. As a father, he is absolutely bewildered. Then, as a look of resolve crosses his face, he says, "Chava is dead to us. We'll forget her. Go home."

Now in the story, his daughter is not really dead, but she is dead to him. And according to the custom of his day, she will not be spoken of again and she will not be welcomed into his home because she is reckoned as dead and her father will consciously resist any memory of her.

In the same way, the disciple of Christ must consider the old sin nature as dead since "we have died with Christ" (v. 8). Therefore, we must continually count, or reckon, this to be so by embracing the reality of our position in Christ by faith. Just as Tevye rejected his daughter, we must reject the flesh. We must not welcome it into our homes. We must not let sin reign in our mortal bodies in order to obey its lusts (v. 12). We must stop presenting the members of our bodies to sin, and instead present ourselves "to God as those alive from the dead" (v. 13). The old man must be dead to us! Likewise, we must consider ourselves alive to God. Since believers have been made "partakers of the divine nature" (2 Peter 1:4), our new nature, empowered by the Holy Spirit, has the capacity to live free from sin's enslavement. "But now having been freed from sin and enslaved to God, you derive your benefit, resulting in sanctification, and the outcome, eternal life" (Rom. 6:22).

God's law drives us to Christ
In case his readers are tempted to view the restrictions of the Law as the cure for their ongoing battle against sin, Paul moves on to deal with that misconception (Rom. 7:1–6). His main point is that the Law can only govern the living. Therefore, since the believer is dead to sin, the Law is not the answer. The Law is powerless to convert the soul (v. 4), control sinful passions (v. 5), or change the inner person (v. 6). However, this does not mean that the Law is bad. On the contrary, God's Law is good because it exposes our sinfulness, which is our core problem (v. 7). It is *sin* that uses the Law to its advantage and seeks to kill spiritual life by cursing us when we fail to live up to its standard (vv. 8–12). The purpose of the Law is to drive us to Jesus Christ where we find perfect righteousness by faith. That is Paul's point in Philippians 3:8–9:

> More than that, I count all things to be loss in view of the surpassing value of knowing Christ Jesus my Lord, for whom I have suffered the loss of all things, and count them but rubbish so that I may gain Christ, and may be found in Him, not having a righteousness of my own derived from the Law, but that

which is through faith in Christ, the righteousness which comes from God on the basis of faith.

The Law is not evil—it is good and holy—but it is inadequate to deal with the heart problem of man. That is why Jesus came. The Law confronts sin, but it cannot change the sinner. That is the work of the gospel!

The source of spiritual struggle

In case his readers still do not understand, Paul makes it even clearer that the Law is not the problem; rather the source of spiritual struggle is the principle of sin that lives within the human heart (vv. 14–24). Here he states three facts, offers proof that each is true, and then draws a conclusion about each one. First, the fact remains that the Law is *spiritual*, but man is fleshly, "sold into bondage to sin" (v. 14). The flesh is the principle of sin that expresses itself through the mind and body. The proof Paul offers is that, at times, he still does what he does not want to do, and does not do what he does want to do (vv. 15–16). His conclusion is that indwelling sin is the root problem: "no longer am I [the new man] the one doing it, but sin which dwells in me" (v. 17).

Second, the fact remains "that nothing good dwells in me," that is, the flesh (v. 18). Paul understands total depravity—that sin has permeated every part of his being. The proof he offers is that he desires to do good, but does not do it. Instead, "I practice the very evil that I do not want" (v. 19). His conclusion is the same: sin "which dwells in me" (v. 20) is the root problem.

Third, the fact remains "that evil is present in me, the one who wants to do good" (v. 21). The proof Paul offers is the war that is raging in the members of his body (vv. 22–23). His conclusion is that indwelling sin is the root problem: "the law of sin which is in my members" (v. 23).

Three times Paul presents the reality of the believer's ongoing struggle to become holy. All three times, his conclusion is the same: indwelling sin is the root problem. Schreiner writes, "Conflict with sin continues even though the lordship of sin has been shattered."[24] But that is not the end of the story.

The source of spiritual victory

The glorious news of the gospel is that, although the disciple of Christ continues to fight a difficult battle against sin and, with the apostle, may often cry out, "Wretched man that I am! Who will set me free from the body of this death?" (v. 24), the final victory of redemption is on its way. With Paul we can confidently shout, "Thanks be to God through Jesus Christ our Lord!" (v. 25). The final victory will come through Christ when He delivers us from our body of sin and death. Sin, which works through the human body, bringing it to death, will eventually be defeated at the resurrection. "The sting of death is sin, and the power of sin is the law; but thanks be to God, who gives us the victory through our Lord Jesus Christ. Therefore, my beloved brethren, be steadfast, immovable, always abounding in the work of the Lord, knowing that your toil is not in vain in the Lord" (1 Cor. 15:56–58).

Discipline the habits of life (1 Peter 1:15–16; 2:1–3)

Finally, the believer's call to the discipline of godliness demands the transformation of lifelong habits through the application of practical righteousness. Peter resumes his call to godliness with a specific exhortation to be like God: "like the Holy One who called you, be holy yourselves also in all your behavior" (1:15). Why? Because "it is written, 'You shall be holy, for I am holy.'" Here he quotes directly from Leviticus 11:44, which is part of God's call to Israel to be distinct from the rest of the nations in order to be a reflection of His true, holy nature. Therefore, a basic understanding of the holiness of God is essential if we are to live up to our holy calling. The holiness of God is His "set-apart-ness." Kent Hughes is correct when he writes, "Holiness is essential to God's nature; it is not so much an attribute of God as it is the very foundation of his being. Holiness denotes the separateness or otherness of God."[25] Holiness is what makes God distinct from His creation. God declared to Moses, "there is no one like Me in all the earth" (Exod. 9:14).

The Greek word translated "holy" in the New Testament is that which means "separate, marked off."[26] It is the same word used for "saints," referring to believers as those who have been set apart by God for Himself. Our occupation is to be "children of obedience" since God has "called us with a holy calling" (2 Tim. 1:9). Alva J. McClain comments on the believer's designation as a saint:

> A Christian whose life is not what it ought to be often gives the excuse: "I don't pretend to be a saint!" It doesn't matter what you pretend to be—if you are a Christian, you are a saint! It is not an evidence of humility to refuse to be

called a saint. It is not humility to refuse to take that name that God has given us but unbelief, masquerading in the role of humility … God never goes to a sinner and tells him to try to attain to sainthood. He picks us out of the mud, and He says, "You are a saint." We are not making believe. We are holy and must live in accordance with our position.[27]

Therefore, when the Scriptures say that we are called to be holy, this is primarily what it means: to be holy is to live in such a way that we accurately reflect God to unregenerate sinners. This does not mean being different for difference's sake, nor drawing attention to ourselves by means of some uniformed appearance, but it means seeking to become like the God who saved us, which naturally results in a life characterized by distinctiveness. Wayne Grudem explains, "The idea of holiness for God's people includes not simply a concept of 'separation' in general but a specifically moral sense of separation *from evil* and dedication *to a life of righteousness.*"[28] This is why Peter compels us to be holy in all our *behavior,* our conduct, our active life; especially "in relation to others."[29] One commentator says that this means we should make holiness our "trademark";[30] in other words, godliness should be our reputation in the world.

This sober approach to the Christian life is an expected response of the believer to the gracious salvation God has provided in Christ. If we have been saved by the grace of God from a life of sin and destruction, then our present calling is to let that same grace empower us to live in such a way that we reflect the righteousness of God to an unrighteous world. For this reason, we must pursue a complete transformation of life which proceeds from the renewal of the mind and the reformation of inner desires to the replacement of sinful habits with the practical working of righteous behavior. This requires the constant application of holiness by putting off the old man and putting on the new.

PUT OFF SIN AND PUT ON RIGHTEOUSNESS

The put off/put on passages of the New Testament are essential to the ministry of authentic biblical counseling since they teach that a large part of sanctification involves the replacing of old sinful habits with new godly ones. This principle is taught in a number of key passages.

Chapter 4

Ephesians 4:25–32

> Therefore, laying aside falsehood, speak truth each one of you with his neighbor, for we are members of one another. Be angry, and yet do not sin; do not let the sun go down on your anger, and do not give the devil an opportunity. He who steals must steal no longer; but rather he must labor, performing with his own hands what is good, so that he will have something to share with one who has need. Let no unwholesome word proceed from your mouth, but only such a word as is good for edification according to the need of the moment, so that it will give grace to those who hear. Do not grieve the Holy Spirit of God, by whom you were sealed for the day of redemption. Let all bitterness and wrath and anger and clamor and slander be put away from you, along with all malice. Be kind to one another, tender-hearted, forgiving each other, just as God in Christ also has forgiven you.

This portion from Ephesians is the most extensive passage that teaches what is often referred to as "the replacement principle."[31] Believers are called upon to stop walking in the old ways of their unsaved past, which were futile. In place of sinful habits, believers must be renewed in their minds— their thinking must change—so that they may habitually put on the new self, "which in the likeness of God has been created in righteousness and holiness of the truth" (Eph. 4:24). The apostle then provides numerous examples of old sinful habits and the corresponding righteous habits that must take their place in the life that is worthy of the calling of God in Christ.

Colossians 3:8–14

> But now you also, put them all aside: anger, wrath, malice, slander, and abusive speech from your mouth. Do not lie to one another, since you laid aside the old self with its evil practices, and have put on the new self who is being renewed to a true knowledge according to the image of the One who created him—a renewal in which there is no distinction between Greek and Jew, circumcised and uncircumcised, barbarian, Scythian, slave and freeman, but Christ is all, and in all. So, as those who have been chosen of God, holy and beloved, put on a heart of compassion, kindness, humility, gentleness and patience; bearing with one another, and forgiving each other, whoever has a complaint against anyone; just as the Lord forgave you, so also should you. Beyond all these things put on love, which is the perfect bond of unity.

Again, the Apostle Paul taught the Colossians that believers are responsible to put off sinful responses such as "anger, wrath, malice, slander, and abusive speech," along with lying and the "evil practices" of the old self. In place of these old habits, believers must put on the new self, "who is being renewed to a true knowledge according to the image of the One who created him." As believers put on the new self by obedience to the Word, they are increasingly conformed by the Spirit into the image of their Creator, Jesus Christ, which is God's goal for every believer (Rom. 8:29). The specific "clothing of God" that believers must discipline themselves to put on includes a "heart of compassion, kindness, humility, gentleness and patience; bearing with one another, and forgiving each other … Beyond all these things put on love, which is the perfect bond of unity."

Hebrews 12:1–2

> Therefore, since we have so great a cloud of witnesses surrounding us, let us also lay aside every encumbrance and the sin which so easily entangles us, and let us run with endurance the race that is set before us, fixing our eyes on Jesus, the author and perfecter of faith, who for the joy set before Him endured the cross, despising the shame, and has sat down at the right hand of the throne of God.

In this passage, we learn that the Christian life is continually both defensive and offensive. We must constantly put off the sin that hinders our growth, weighing us down from within, and put on righteous habits that help us win the spiritual race. Jesus is our example of running the race of holiness and fulfilling the will of God.

1 Peter 2:1–3

> Therefore, putting aside all malice and all deceit and hypocrisy and envy and all slander, like newborn babies, long for the pure milk of the word, so that by it you may grow in respect to salvation, if you have tasted the kindness of the Lord.

Returning to the book of First Peter, we notice the second chapter progresses from the apostle's call to renew our minds and repent of former lusts to applying practical righteousness. Peter's words stress that the key to godliness is the constant application of the Word of God to our lives, whereby we are continually doing two things: putting off the sin that so easily entangles us and putting on the righteousness that is the character of Christ.

CAST AWAY THE SINS THAT HINDER GROWTH

If we as disciples want to experience steady growth in the Lord, we must cast away the sins that hinder us from making progress in spiritual growth. Staying with the passage quoted above from 1 Peter 2, we see that "Therefore" (2:1) connects us to three key truths that Peter has expounded in his previous chapter: at salvation, believers obeyed the truth (1:22), were born again by God (1:23), and were saved by the power of the imperishable Word (1:23–24).

The Greek word translated "putting aside" (2:1) is applied to any kind of rejection, especially one that is connected in any way to person, body, or mind.[32] In other words, there are sinful life-patterns that must be rejected. It is in the middle voice, which means that this is what we must do ourselves. It could be translated, "You yourselves be continually putting these sins away from yourselves." In other words, nobody else can do this for us. We must actively put aside or reject sin. The Puritan Thomas Watson said, "If we could see hell fire in every sin, it would make us fear to commit [it]. The fiercest creatures dread fire. When Moses' rod was turned into a serpent he was afraid and fled from it. Sin will prove to be a stinging serpent. Oh, fly from it!"[33] The more we focus on the holiness of God, the more we will hate our sin, just as Solomon wrote, "The fear of the LORD is to hate evil" (Prov. 8:13).

Peter then gives five examples of the sins that we must actively reject. Again, as we saw in Chapter 3, the list of sins is not exhaustive, but merely representative of the kinds of behaviors that biblical counselors will need to help people change.

Malice

"Malice" is an all-inclusive term for wickedness,[34] and describes our unsaved past: "For we also once were foolish ourselves, disobedient, deceived, enslaved to various lusts and pleasures, spending our life in malice and envy, hateful, hating one another" (Titus 3:3). In other words, we were pursuing sin, not God. We were children of His wrath (Eph. 2:3). Jerry Bridges says it well: "The truly godly person never forgets that he was at one time an object of God's holy and just wrath."[35] Remembering that we were once "separate from Christ" (Eph. 2:12) will properly motivate us toward holiness out of love for our Savior (2 Cor. 5:14–15).

Ephesians 4:31–32 affirms the putting off of malice: "Let all bitterness and wrath and anger and clamor and slander be put away from you, along with all malice. And be kind to one another, tender-hearted, forgiving each other, just as God in Christ also has forgiven you." The virtues of kindness and forgiveness are to be put in place of the sins of anger and malice and their close relative, bitterness. A bitter person is usually someone who refuses to forgive others or one who will not humbly submit to God's sovereignty through the painful trials of life. Therefore, the author of Hebrews identifies bitterness as a shortage of grace. "See to it that no one comes short of the grace of God; that no root of bitterness springing up causes trouble, and by it many be defiled" (Heb. 12:15).

Deceit

In addition to putting off malice, believers are to put away "deceit." In the Greek, the word comes from a verb meaning "to catch with bait."[36] It is the picture of the fisherman who reads all the sportsmen magazines and makes all necessary preparations to bait his hook. Or it is like the hunter who thoroughly researches the animal he is targeting. He learns what kinds of food it likes to eat, its sleep patterns, and its life habits, so that he knows how, when, and where to position himself at any given time of day. The same kind of picture is painted by the Gospel writers in their descriptions of the scribes and Pharisees as those who were seeking to trap Jesus. This kind of premeditated deceit has no place in the life of a godly person. Psalm 32:2 says, "How blessed is the man to whom the LORD does not impute iniquity, and in whose spirit there is no deceit!" In other words, we are to put off deceit. How? By learning the new habit of speaking truth. "Therefore, *laying aside falsehood, speak truth* each one of you with his neighbor, for we are members of one another" (Eph. 4:25). As we consciously repent of deceit and replace this ungodly habit with a commitment to always speak truth, even when it is inconvenient or personally sacrificial, we are putting on the new self and learning to act in love toward others.

Hypocrisy

Peter also urged his readers to put off "hypocrisy." Kenneth Wuest explains the New Testament use of this word:

> The true identity of the person is covered up. It refers to acts of impersonation or deception. It was used of an actor on the Greek stage. Taken over into the New Testament, it referred to a person we call a hypocrite, one who assumes the mannerisms, speech, and character of someone else, thus hiding his true identity. Christianity requires that believers should be open and above-board. They should be themselves. Their lives should be like an open book, easily read.37

Jesus warns, "Beware of the leaven of the Pharisees, which is hypocrisy" (Luke 12:1). He said this because the Pharisees were professional hypocrites. They wore the mask of spirituality, but inside they were full of dead men's bones. As disciple-makers, the Pharisees were content to make people look acceptable on the outside while remaining grotesque on the inside. Jesus, therefore, uses strong language to denounce hypocrisy, and issues forth woes:

> But woe to you, scribes and Pharisees, hypocrites, because you shut off the kingdom of heaven from people; for you do not enter in yourselves, nor do you allow those who are entering to go in. Woe to you, scribes and Pharisees, hypocrites, because you devour widows' houses, and for a pretense you make long prayers; therefore you will receive greater condemnation. Woe to you, scribes and Pharisees, hypocrites, because you travel around on sea and land to make one proselyte; and when he becomes one, you make him twice as much a son of hell as yourselves.
>
> Matt. 23:13–15

To make a person "twice as much a son of hell" as a Pharisee is to make him moral, but not regenerate. That is, it is more difficult to lead that person to true salvation because, through hypocrisy, he or she has learned to conform to an outward "form of godliness, although [denying] its power" (2 Tim. 3:5). Sinners do not need morality. They need the gospel of Jesus Christ! And when they have Christ, morality will follow.

Envy

"Envy" means "the feeling of displeasure produced by witnessing or hearing of the advantage or prosperity of others."[38] The psalmist confessed, "But as for me, my feet came close to stumbling, my steps had almost slipped. For I was envious of the arrogant, as I saw the prosperity of the wicked" (Ps. 73:2–3). In the New Testament, envy always carries an evil sense. For example, Matthew informs us that it was "because of envy" that the angry crowd delivered up Jesus to Pilate (27:18). Galatians 5:21 says that envy is one of the fruits of the flesh. When envy is present, we know without a doubt that we are not under the control of the Holy Spirit, but rather of the flesh. There are three means of overcoming envy.

First, since envy feeds on ingratitude, it is necessary to nurture a thankful heart. Scripture exhorts, "in everything give thanks; for this is God's will for you in Christ Jesus" (1 Thes. 5:18). Second, guarding our hearts from envy also includes cultivating contentment—being satisfied with what God has given us. "If we have food and covering, with these we shall be content" (1 Tim. 6:8). Paul's own personal testimony was that he had "learned to be content in whatever circumstances" he was in (Phil. 4:11). Third, to replace envy with practical righteousness we must also learn to rejoice with other believers when their blessings seem to exceed our own. Through self-discipline, we must strive to replace selfish feelings of displeasure with those of rejoicing so that we can indeed "Rejoice with those who rejoice" (Rom. 12:15). Learning to nurture this kind of heart will empower us to put off envy.

Slander

The word translated "slander" is from a combination of two words meaning "down" and "speak," thus giving the meaning "to speak down about someone." It is translated "evil speaking" in the New King James Version. Louis Barbieri defines slander as "any communication that runs down someone or attempts to belittle another person."[39] According to Proverbs 20:19, slander includes the blabbering of secrets as well as gossip: "He who goes about as a slanderer reveals secrets, therefore do not associate with a gossip." Gossip and slander go hand in hand, as Wayne Mack notes in his book *Your Family God's Way*:

> People who carry gossip to you will often carry gossip *about* you as well. At first, you may think you are privileged in having this person share private information with you. Later you discover that you have been "had," because

you find out that this same person has been spreading evil reports about you to other people.⁴⁰

Slander is a sin that must be deliberately put off since the tongue is a powerful muscle and the most difficult to control (James 3:8). However, slander is not primarily a tongue problem. Jesus warns that slander comes forth "out of the heart" (Matt. 15:19). Therefore, the inner change that is needed is to "fervently love one another from the heart" (1 Peter 1:22) and "with humility of mind regard one another as more important than yourselves" (Phil. 2:3). James 4:11 warns, "Do not speak against one another, brethren," which is another way of saying, "put away slander."

These are five examples of sins that will hinder our spiritual growth if not rejected. Therefore, biblical counselors will need to help disciples learn to put away these and other heart sins. But there is another side to godliness—what we must put on, or crave.

CRAVE THE WORD THAT PROMOTES GROWTH

As ingrained sin habits are being cast aside, the follower of Christ must also develop the new habit of craving His Word so that he or she may do all things that Jesus commanded. Like newly born nursing babes, we need to have an intense desire for the pure, uncontaminated Word of God. Peter says that if we "long for" it, we will grow (1 Peter 2:2). Scripture is the instrumental cause of saving faith (Rom. 10:17). However, it is also the instrumental cause of our growth in godliness. Therefore, believers with a small appetite for the Scriptures experience limited growth. But those with a strong appetite for the Word and a hunger and thirst for God's truth become growing Christians as they apply its truth to life. Job's godly testimony was "I have not departed from the command of His lips; I have treasured the words of His mouth more than my necessary food" (Job 23:12). James 1:21 urges believers, "Therefore, putting aside all filthiness and all that remains of wickedness, in humility receive the word implanted, which is able to save your souls."

However, in order for this ongoing sanctification to take place, we must have godly appetites. Think with me for a moment. What is your appetite for food like? Now compare that to your appetite for the Word of God. Do you treasure Scripture more than food? Do you delight in it? Jeremiah 6:10

says of the wicked, "Behold, their ears are closed and they cannot listen. Behold, the word of the Lord has become a reproach to them; they have no delight in it." In contrast, the prophet's personal testimony was "Your words were found and I ate them, and Your words became for me a joy and the delight of my heart" (Jer. 15:16). In order to crave a steady diet of the Word, we need to discipline ourselves for two kinds of intake: personal and public.

Personal intake

Personal intake of the Word requires daily meditation and study. The blessed man is the one who rejects the counsel of the world because his habit of delighting in the law of the Lord causes him to meditate on it day and night. This results in spiritual growth and fruitfulness (Ps. 1:1–3). Peter indicates that our relationship to the Word of God is a key part of our growth "in respect to salvation" (1 Peter 2:2). This is not growing *into* being saved, but rather speaks of growth as the *outworking* of salvation that has already been received in the heart. In other words, since we have experienced God's salvation, "tasted the kindness of God," then we must crave the Word that will make us grow. In light of this, John Piper's words are especially challenging: "Our approach to the Bible should be like a miser in the gold rush, or a fiancée who has lost her engagement ring somewhere in the house."[41] That is what our attitude toward the Scriptures ought to be like! The psalmist also understood the connection between delighting in the Word and his walk of obedience and therefore prayed, "Make me walk in the path of Your commandments, for I delight in it" (119:35).

Public intake

The growing disciple is also one who places a high priority on listening to the public reading and preaching of the Word of God. Paul warned Timothy that the last days will be a time when "men will be lovers of self" (2 Tim. 3:2) and, therefore, professing Christians will turn their ears away from sound preaching toward man-centered myths that tickle their ears (2 Tim. 4:1–4). In contrast, faithful followers of Jesus make participation in public worship services a high priority for themselves and their families as they involve themselves in the lives of their local churches. They do not forsake their local assemblies, "as is the habit of some" (Heb. 10:25), but instead they delight in gathering for corporate worship and fellowship so that they may hear the preaching of God's Word and encourage one another to press on toward becoming like Jesus, whose return they eagerly await.

Summary

Continual progress in discipleship is a lifelong journey toward becoming like the Holy One who called us by His sanctifying grace. However, the self-glorifying sin principle that remains within our bodies demands that we intensively apply personal discipline toward the renewal of our minds, repentance from depraved lusts, and replacement of ungodly habits with the godliness of Christ—into whose image we will one day be fully remade. James Boice writes,

> The Christian life is not easy. No responsible person ever said it was. It is a battle all the way. But it is a battle that will be won. And when it is won, we who have triumphed will cast our crowns at the feet of the Lord Jesus Christ, who worked in us to accomplish the victory, and we will praise Him forever.[42]

Since the Christian life is a difficult war, there will be times when some soldiers get wounded on the battlefield and therefore need the extra care that loving disciple-makers provide. When this happens, a biblical plan must be activated. Now let us examine God's plan for the restoration of fallen disciples.

For further thought and small-group discussion

1. Read 2 Peter 1:5–10. Discuss the importance of personal discipline in the process of growing in godliness. Discuss the common misconceptions that some believers have concerning their role in the process of sanctification (mentioned at the beginning of this chapter). Have you been guilty of any of these misunderstandings?

2. Read 1 Peter 1:13–16. Discuss God's call to holiness and your personal responsibility to become like Christ. What does the Holy Spirit want you to change?

3. Read Romans 12:1–2. Discuss the connection between the "renewing of your mind" and being transformed by the power of God.

4. Read James 4:1–3. Discuss the role that lusts of the heart play in personal conflicts with others. Discuss the importance of asking ourselves, when angry, "What is it that my sinful heart craves so much that I am willing to commit murder in my heart to get it?"

5. Read Romans 7:14–25. Discuss the problem of indwelling sin and the victory that is ours in Jesus Christ. What key truths from Romans 6 and 7 do you need to refresh your mind with daily?

6. Read Ephesians 4:25–32. Discuss how "the replacement principle" affects personal godliness. What is the logical reasoning upon which Paul bases his instruction? What examples does he give in this passage? What sinful habits do you need to replace with righteous ones?

7. Read John 17:17. What role does the written Word of God have in our sanctification? What changes does the Holy Spirit want you to make concerning your *private* and *public* intake of the Word?

The compassion of brotherly love

Chapter 5

Brethren, even if anyone is caught in any trespass, you who are spiritual, restore such a one in a spirit of gentleness; each one looking to yourself, so that you too will not be tempted. Bear one another's burdens, and thereby fulfill the law of Christ. For if anyone thinks he is something when he is nothing, he deceives himself. But each one must examine his own work, and then he will have reason for boasting in regard to himself alone, and not in regard to another. For each one will bear his own load.

–Gal. 6:1–5

Authentic biblical counseling lives out God's redeeming love through believers as we take initiative to restore brothers and sisters who are experiencing spiritual defeat in the battle with indwelling sin. God's vision of discipleship requires a commitment to help those trapped by sin's power in order that these "strugglers" might learn to walk in newness of the Spirit as obedient followers of Jesus Christ. For that reason, we must accept that the process of discipleship will get messy at times, because sin damages everything it touches and hurts everyone it traps. Because of this reality, those who have made the commitment to love biblically must always be prepared to minister the compassion of Christ and rescue those in bondage.

We should begin by making an observation. While some counseling situations are initiated by counselees when they finally recognize that they are trapped and cannot get out of sin's bondage without help, other counseling relationships are initiated by biblical counselors as a result of observing foolish choices or sinful life patterns in brothers or sisters in Christ. Whether or not the ensnared brothers or sisters see that they are in bondage is not the issue. Love initiates the restoration of strugglers to a place of fellowship and blessing. William Goode, long-time pastor of Faith Baptist Church in Lafayette, Indiana and founder of Faith Baptist Counseling Ministry, compellingly writes that

> to consider counseling an optional ministry is to withhold biblical love at the
> time it is needed most in the believer's life—when he or she is in trouble … we

must be about the business of restoring rather than ignoring such Christians … Believers will never become like Christ if they are not winning the battle against sin in their lives and investing themselves in the lives of others. And there can be no discipling if there is no plan to help the disciple who gets into trouble.[1]

Galatians 6:1–5 provides such a plan.

The presuppositions of biblical counseling

The Apostle Paul begins this text with three basic presuppositions. Understanding these principles will help biblical counselors approach the process of restoring fallen brethren in a way that exemplifies the love of Christ.

BIBLICAL COUNSELING PRESUPPOSES A SPIRITUAL RELATIONSHIP

The first word in the text is significant. "Brethren" indicates that counseling is a family matter: that is, a ministry of discipleship within the family of God. In fact, that is what the church is—a visible family of the invisible God. The New Testament most commonly refers to believers in familial terms such as "brethren," "brother," or "sister," which occur some 250 times. The church is the original "brotherhood" (1 Peter 2:17). This analogy has numerous implications. For example, it obligates us to "Be devoted to one another" (Rom. 12:10), to care for one another's needs (Acts 2:44–45; 4:32; 11:29–30; 1 John 3:17–18; 1 Tim. 5:1–16), and to pray for one another (James 5:13–16). However, the familial commitment of the brotherhood also requires us to exhort, and if necessary, discipline family members who are in sin. The Bible's plan for restoration is carried out *by* brethren *for* brethren.

BIBLICAL COUNSELING PRESUPPOSES A SPIRITUAL PROBLEM

The phrase "… if a man is caught in any trespass" indicates that something has happened and now it is time for personal restorative ministry to begin. It is the picture of the man or woman who has been overtaken by surprise, "before one can escape."[2] This spiritual defeat is caused by a "trespass," that is, "a false step, a blunder,"[3] which reminds us of the nature of sin to deceive and ensnare. Thomas Watson's book is appropriately entitled *The Mischief of Sin*. In it he reminds us,

> Sin first tempts and then damns. It is first a fox and then a lion. Sin does to a man as Jael did to Sisera. She gave him milk, but then she brought him low.

Judges 5:26–27, "She put her hand to the nail, and with the hammer she smote Sisera, she smote off his head; when she had pierced and stricken through his temples, at her feet he bowed." Sin first brings us pleasures which delight and charm the senses, and then comes with its nail and hammer. Sin does to the sinner as Absalom did to Amnon. When his heart was merry with wine, then he killed him, 2 Samuel 13:28. Sin's last act is always tragic.4

When fellow believers give in to sin's power and step aside from God's path, they need our loving help to get back into fellowship with Him and with others they may have sinned against, before destruction occurs. Biblical counseling may often be the emergency room and the intensive care unit of the discipleship hospital. When a part of the body has been hurt by sinful choices, that member needs to be taken aside into more personalized care for the purpose of "heart surgery" and "rehabilitation."

BIBLICAL COUNSELING PRESUPPOSES A SPIRITUAL GOAL

The goal of this personal ministry is to "restore such a one," which must always be the objective. Sinning brothers and sisters need their fellowship with God restored through repentance toward God and reconciliation with others through confession and forgiveness. The word used for "restore" is a medical term referring to the setting of a broken bone. According to Ephesians 4:12, where the same term is translated "equipping," pastor-teachers must train others in the church to do the work of ministry by equipping them to love each other enough to confront one another when necessary. Too many believers think that this ministry of confrontation belongs exclusively to their pastor, but that is not the case. This kind of targeted discipleship requires a commitment from every believer to not cast away or abandon brothers or sisters who are struggling with spiritual defeat (or farm them out to a professional counselor5). Instead we must actively come alongside them in order to set the broken bones of their hearts and minds, teach them how to get back on God's path and thereby train them to consistently walk in His way. Dr. Paul Brand describes the healing process of a fracture in his and Philip Yancey's book *Fearfully and Wonderfully Made*, which serves as a fitting illustration of how the body of Christ should function:

> When bone breaks, an elaborate process begins. Excited repair cells invade in swarms. Within two weeks a cartilage-like sheath called callus surrounds

the region and cement-laying cells enter the jellied mass. These cells are the osteoblasts, the pothole-fillers of the bone. Gradually they break down the callus and replace it with fresh bone. In two or three months the fracture site is marked by a mass of new bone that bulges over both sides of the broken ends like a spliced garden hose. Later, surplus material is scavenged so the final result nearly matches the original bone. That is bone's normal healing cycle.[6]

Just as God marvelously designed the human body to heal a broken bone, so He has equipped the body of Christ with all that is necessary for every member to be involved in the process of restoring broken parts damaged by sin. As with the human body's reaction to broken bone, restoration of sinning brethren should be the "normal healing cycle." The goal of restoration to the Lord, which includes reconciliation with the family of God, is consistently taught by other Scriptures:

- "Therefore if you are presenting your offering at the altar, and there remember that your brother has something against you, leave your offering there before the altar and go; *first be reconciled to your brother*, and then come and present your offering" (Matt. 5:23–24).

- "If your brother sins, go and show him his fault in private; if he listens to you, *you have won your brother*. But if he does not listen to you, take one or two more with you, so that by the mouth of two or three witnesses every fact may be confirmed. If he refuses to listen to them, tell it to the church; and if he refuses to listen even to the church, let him be to you as a Gentile and a tax collector" (Matt. 18:15–17).

- "My brethren, if any among you strays from the truth and one turns him back, let him know that he who turns a sinner from the error of his way will save his soul from death and will cover a multitude of sins" (James 5:19–20).

- "It is for discipline that you endure; God deals with you as with sons; for what son is there whom his father does not discipline? But if you are without discipline, of which all have become partakers, then you are illegitimate children and not sons. Furthermore, we had earthly fathers to discipline us, and we respected them; shall we not much rather be subject to the Father of spirits, and live? For they disciplined us for a short time as seemed best to them, but He disciplines us for our good, so that we may share His holiness. All discipline for the moment seems not to be joyful, but sorrowful; yet to those who have been trained by it, afterwards it yields the peaceful fruit of righteousness" (Heb. 12:7–11).

In all of these passages, the goal is the same. It is always restorative and never punitive. In particular, we conclude from the passage in Hebrews that God does not punish His children—He disciplines them. There is an enormous difference between punishment and discipline, which is summarizd in the chart on the following page.

Punishment casts away, while discipline restores. Punishment is for subjects of wrath, while discipline is for children of God. Punishment requires payment for sin, while discipline corrects to protect and bless, because sin has already been paid for by Jesus. Punishment focuses on past sins, whereas discipline, while still dealing with sin, looks to the future blessing of obedience that follows true repentance. This is why punishment often provokes believers to wrath while biblical discipline works to produce sorrow leading to repentance.

Understanding the difference between judicial punishment and parental discipline is crucial to being effective in the discipleship process. God is our example. He never punishes His children. He does not give us tally marks for misconduct. Instead, He does the harder work of coming alongside offenders, confronting them in love, leading them to repentance and biblical confession, and restoring them to fellowship so that they may continue to be sanctified. The main reason why a punitive approach to sanctification does not work is because it fails to adequately address the issue of the heart—where true change begins. Most seriously, it risks undermining one's comprehension of and confidence in the atonement of Christ, who took all our punishment on the cross. This is more than semantics! How discipline is handled in the discipleship process either affirms the theology of the cross or subtly replaces it with a performance-based approach to godliness that may feed a fear of man as the motivation for holiness rather than the infinitely superior drive of love for Christ: "and He died for all, that they who live should no longer live for themselves, but for Him who died and rose again on their behalf" (2 Cor. 5:15).

A THEOLOGY OF DISCIPLINE		
	PUNISHMENT	**DISCIPLINE**
Nature	**punitive** "I will punish the world for its evil, and the wicked for their iniquity." (Isa. 13:11)	**corrective** "... but He disciplines us for our good ..." (Heb. 12:10)
Motivation	**anger, wrath, hatred** "Behold, the day of the Lord is coming, cruel, with fury and burning anger." (Isa. 13:9)	**love, responsibility, grief over sin** "For those whom the Lord loves he disciplines, and he scourges every son whom he receives." (Heb. 12:6)
Goal	**to inflict penalty, to require payment for sin** "... dealing out retribution to those who do not know God and to those who do not obey the gospel of our Lord Jesus." (2 Thes. 1:8)	**to correct, protect, and bless** "My son, do not forget my teaching, but let your heart keep my commandments; for length of days and years of life and peace they will add to you." (Prov. 3:1–2)
View	**dwells on the past** "... the Lord will repay him according to his deeds." (2 Tim. 4:14)	**hopes in the future** "... so that we may share His holiness." (Heb. 12:10)
Common response	**resentment leading to bitterness** "... men blasphemed God because of the plague ..." (Rev. 16:21)	**sorrow leading to repentance** "All discipline for the moment seems not to be joyful, but sorrowful ..." (Heb. 12:11a)
Result in the relationship	**abandonment/isolation** "These will go away into eternal punishment ..." (Matt. 25:46)	**reconciliation/restoration** "But if you are without discipline, of which all have become partakers, then you are illegitimate children and not sons." (Heb. 12:8)
End	**destruction** "These will pay the penalty of eternal destruction, away from the presence of the Lord and from the glory of His power ..." (2 Thes. 1:9)	**change of character** "... yet to those who have been trained by it, afterwards it yields the peaceful fruit of righteousness." (Heb. 12:11b)

The biblical disciple-maker must be committed to the same goal to which God is committed—the restoration of His sinning child to a place of fellowship, obedience, and blessing. There certainly may come a time when the disciple-maker must let his or her pupil defiantly walk away from the biblical help being offered. However, until then, the one who is "spiritual" must practice this kind of loving confrontation, modeling God's relationship to His children and creating a grace-dispensing environment for believers to grow in.

The qualifications of the biblical counselor

Paul makes it clear that those who lead the confrontation of restoring love must be "spiritual." This is a translation of *pneumatikos* and in this context it refers to "men in Christ who walk so as to please God."7 In other words, men and women who are walking and growing in the Spirit are those who are qualified to come alongside sinning brothers and sisters to gently restore them to the spiritual blessing that flows from obedience. Without the Holy Spirit, biblical counseling cannot exist. He is the divine counselor Jesus promised to send (John 14:16). As disciples submit their hearts to the Lord, the Spirit not only causes them to grow in godliness, but also equips them to be His instruments of change in the lives of others.

The responsibilities of the biblical counselor

Our passage from Galatians also reveals three responsibilities biblical counselors must fulfill in carrying out the personal ministry of restoring sinning brethren to an obedient walk of faith.

RESTORE GENTLY, WITH GRACE

First, restoration must be done "in a spirit of gentleness" (Gal. 6:1). In other words, no allowance is made for a harsh, judgmental, or critical spirit. As we as counselors learn to walk in the Spirit, we will display the fruit of gentleness (Gal. 5:23), which in turn will be used by God to reach the hearts of those we are trying to help. Paul David Tripp is correct when he writes,

> Gentleness should be our natural response when we see a brother or sister ensnared in sin. We must recognize that except for God's grace, we would be where they are. Thus we should respond to them with the same grace we have received. God loved us when we were unlovely. He has forgiven us in

the face of repeated sin. In fact, it is His love that draws us out of the darkness toward His marvelous light. In our communication with one another, as we all struggle with the reality of remaining sin, it is vital that we mirror the compelling love of Christ.[8]

Even in the case of disciplining a stiff-necked man, who has to be disassociated from because of his refusal to obey apostolic instruction, Paul encourages the believers to "not regard him as an enemy, but admonish him as a brother" (2 Thes. 3:14–15). The familial bond in Christ dictates how a sinning family member is to be treated—with grace.

Restore Humbly, with Self-examination

Second, the ministry of restoring a sinning brother or sister must be done in a spirit of humility, "each one looking to yourself, so that you too will not be tempted" (v. 1). Biblical humility understands that even the most mature believer is still susceptible to the incredible power of the evil temptations resident in the human heart (James 1:13–14). "For if anyone thinks he is something when he is nothing, he deceives himself" (Gal. 6:3). As we disciple others to follow Christ in obedience, we must always keep a close eye on our own hearts. Solomon warned his son, "Watch over your heart with all diligence, for from it flow the springs of life" (Prov. 4:23). Until Jesus returns and we are glorified (1 John 3:2), we must recognize that sin is ever crouching at our door and its desire is for us (Gen. 4:7). A helpful passage to prayerfully meditate on prior to confronting another person is Matthew 7:1–5:

> Do not judge so that you will not be judged. For in the way you judge, you will be judged; and by your standard of measure, it will be measured to you. Why do you look at the speck that is in your brother's eye, but do not notice the log that is in your own eye? Or how can you say to your brother, "Let me take the speck out of your eye," and behold, the log is in your own eye? You hypocrite, first take the log out of your own eye, and then you will see clearly to take the speck out of your brother's eye.

Jesus clearly indicates that the absence of humility and self-examination is an enormous hindrance to the one-another ministry of confrontation. Pride blinds the spiritual eyes of the counselor, thus leading to self-deception.

In contrast, humility creates an atmosphere of love and patience that is essential to meeting the goal of restoration.

RESTORE SUPPORTIVELY, WITH ACCOUNTABILITY

Third, the exhortation "Bear one another's burdens" (v. 2) means that the ministry of restoration involves helping carry the weight of another person's sin. The "burden" in this context is the weight of sin or the "burden of temptations"9 that has trapped sinning brothers or sisters. To bear this weight is to help them carry their sin burden. Richard Baxter encouraged his fellow pastors to serve their sheep in this way:

> Another class of converts that need our special help, are those who labour under some particular corruption, which keeps under their graces, and makes them a trouble to others, and a burden to themselves. Alas! There are too many such persons. Some are specially addicted to pride, and others to worldly-mindedness; some to sensual desires, and others to frowardness or other evil passions. Now it is our duty to give assistance to all these; and partly by dissuasions, and clear discoveries of the odiousness of sin, and partly by suitable directions about the remedy, to help them to a more complete conquest of their corruptions.10

Nevertheless, though spiritual ones are responsible for carrying the burden *with* them, they do not carry it *for* them: "For each one will bear his own load" (v. 5). In other words, whatever help we give to sinning brothers or sisters must not remove an ounce of personal responsibility, since they are, first and foremost, morally accountable to God as creatures made in His image. While we lovingly confront, in keeping with the goal of restoration, we must remind them that "the law of the Spirit of life in Christ Jesus has set you free from the law of sin and of death" (Rom. 8:2). By ministering in this way, we "fulfill the law of Christ" (Gal. 6:2), who came not to be served but to serve (Mark 10:45).

Summary

Jay Adams, a pioneer in the present-day biblical counseling movement, writes of the priority of love in our relationships with fellow disciples:

> Love for God and one's neighbor constitutes the sum of God's requirements for the Christian. The man who loves needs no counseling. Love cements

relationships between God and man and man and man. While love attracts, fear repels. When love gives, lust grabs. What love builds, hatred destroys. With love communication flourishes; with resentment it withers. Love is the ultimate answer to all the problems of living with which the Christian counselor deals. Love, therefore, is the goal.[11]

As disciple-makers, we must recognize that we are not the only ones fighting the daily battle against sin, but our brothers and sisters are too, though some of them may be losing the war and need extra help in gaining the victory. If walking in love is what we are training disciples for, then we must model this same love throughout the process of making disciples. This means that we must love our brothers and sisters in Christ enough to humbly confront them when they are trapped by sin, and gently lead them into paths of righteousness. Ministry *without* this kind of love profits nothing (1 Cor. 13:1–3). Love looks to the long-term good of the defeated disciple and brings forth compassionate, restorative, humble ministry to a fellow sinner, recognizing that, to one degree or another, we are all "strugglers" and therefore must maintain a commitment to the kind of ministry that restores. As we have seen in this chapter, the Word of God provides a plan for this kind of restoration, which is further testimony of its sufficiency for the ministry of counseling.

For further thought and small-group discussion

1. Read Galatians 6:1–5. Discuss the importance of the word "brethren."

2. Read Ephesians 4:11–16. Discuss the main role of the pastor-teacher. Compare this with Acts 6:1–7. What are your expectations of your pastor? How do they match up with what these passages teach? Are you doing *your part* in building up the body of your church? How often do you pray for your pastor? When was the last time you wrote your pastor an encouraging note to thank him for his ministry in your life?

3. Read Hebrews 12:7–11. Discuss the difference between biblical discipline and punishment as set out in the chart "A theology of discipline."

4. Read Matthew 7:1–5. Discuss the importance of self-examination before confronting other brothers or sisters about their sin. Discuss the importance of accountability in discipleship relationships.

5. Read 1 Corinthians 13:1–7. Discuss the characteristics of biblical love. Does biblical love care enough to confront? Do you love your brother or sister enough to confront him or her? Do you love other believers enough to restore them to fellowship and blessing?

The conviction of the living Word

Chapter 6

All Scripture is inspired by God and profitable for teaching, for reproof, for correction, for training in righteousness; that the man of God may be adequate, equipped for every good work.

–2 Tim. 3:16–17

For the word of God is living and active and sharper than any two-edged sword, and piercing as far as the division of soul and spirit, of both joints and marrow, and able to judge the thoughts and intentions of the heart.

–Heb. 4:12

Authentic biblical counseling chooses no other foundation to build its philosophy and practice upon than the Scriptures: the will of God faithfully revealed to man by the Spirit from the living Word, Jesus Christ. God's vision of discipleship requires a conviction that biblical truth is supremely authoritative and completely adequate for its task. Therefore, we must diligently search the Scriptures in order to know God better and to understand man's needs, as God defines them, so that we may help others experience the transformation of life that characterizes followers of Jesus Christ. First and foremost, this demands an unwavering commitment to the sufficiency of the Scriptures to deal with every soul-related struggle a believer may face during the Spirit's ongoing work of sanctification.

Sadly, the church in the United States, as a whole, does not have this commitment. In his book *The Disciple Making Pastor*, Bill Hull exposed the church's departure from the sufficiency of the written Word of God and its resulting embrace of the principles of psychology:

> The influence of the world's psychology has created a new cult of self-worship. People are preoccupied with themselves and how they might meet society's manufactured set of needs. Psychology exists by putting people in need; people have been told they have needs they never before knew existed. Just as the advertising industry creates false needs in people to go out and spend money on alleged need items, people scramble about trying to meet a new strata of emotional needs manufactured by the psychological industry.

The newscaster gives us the awful truth, which is reality; the Bible gives us the revealed truth, which is revelation; psychology has given us the hidden truth, which is a rip-off. America is the psychological society, and the language and philosophy of need have seduced the church. Therefore, the people in the pew ask all the wrong questions, based on cultural programming: *What can the church do for me? Can I get my needs met here? Do I feel good when I leave here? Does the pastor make me feel guilty? Will I have to do what I don't feel like doing?* These questions and more reflect the corruption of self-idolatry primarily fostered in our society by the secular psychological community.[1]

In light of the biblical priority of teaching and applying sound doctrine, it is distressing to think that, over time, God's people could lose something so basic and essential as the skill and the conviction of the use of Scripture in order to help people work through their personal problems, yet that is where the church is today. Those who embrace psychology as the answer are in the majority by far and there is no reason to pretend they are not. The remedy to the current state of affairs is an uncompromising return to the early church's faith in God's Word as being all-sufficient for the spiritual needs of man.

Sufficiency of the Word (2 Tim. 3:16–17)

Though many believers today are intimidated by mental-health professionals, believers throughout history believed that there is nothing man experiences that God does not directly or indirectly address in His Word, either by precept or principle. Psalm 19:7–9 is an example of their confidence:

> The law of the LORD is perfect, restoring the soul;
> The testimony of the LORD is sure, making wise the simple.
> The precepts of the LORD are right, rejoicing the heart;
> The commandment of the LORD is pure, enlightening the eyes.
> The fear of the LORD is clean, enduring forever;
> The judgments of the LORD are true; they are righteous altogether.

The resource of the Word is rich beyond measure. It is sufficient to deal with every problem man faces because Scripture is the revelation of God, man's Creator, and it is "more desirable than gold" because of its perfection (Ps. 19:10). New Testament believers also had confidence in the Scriptures as being adequate to teach us what to believe and how to live. They believed that the Word confronts us when we get off the right path and shows us how to get back on. Moreover, they believed that the Scriptures train us to live godly lives so that we may mature and become equipped to serve God: "All Scripture is inspired by God and profitable for teaching, for reproof, for correction, for training in righteousness; so that the man of God may be adequate, equipped for every good work" (2 Tim. 3:16–17).

This key text clearly states that the Scriptures are "inspired." Henry Thiessen describes inspiration this way: "The Holy Spirit so guided and superintended the writers of the sacred text, making use of their own unique personalities, that they wrote all that he wanted them to write, without excess or error."[2] Of 2 Timothy 3:16, Wayne Grudem writes,

> Since it is writings that are said to be "breathed out," this breathing must be understood as a metaphor for speaking the words of Scripture. This verse states in brief form what was evident in many passages in the Old Testament: the Old Testament writings are regarded as God's Word in written form. For every word of the Old Testament, God is the one who spoke (and still speaks) it, although God used human agents to write these words down.[3]

Since the Scriptures are breathed out by God, they are "profitable," meaning "useful, beneficial, advantageous."[4] Paul uses the same word in his first letter to Timothy to contrast bodily exercise, which has little benefit, with godliness, which "is profitable for all things" (1 Tim. 4:8). Sound teaching, he instructs, is "good and profitable for all men" (Titus 3:8). According to 2 Timothy 3:16–17, the usefulness of the Bible is demonstrated by four of its functions.

Teaching

"Teaching" refers to doctrine. Scripture instructs us as to what we are to believe about God, about ourselves, and about our Redeemer. Let us not forget Paul's exhortation to Timothy, "Pay close attention to yourself and to your teaching; persevere in these things, for as you do this you will ensure salvation both for yourself and for those who hear you" (1 Tim. 4:16). Even though Timothy was a young pastor, Paul challenged him, "Let no one look down on your youthfulness, but rather in speech, conduct, love, faith and purity, show yourself an example of those who believe" (1 Tim. 4:12).

As biblical counselors, therefore, we must take great care to pay attention to our own lives as well as our theology. As a result, we will be able to teach the way of Christ not only in word, but by example as well. Titus was given the same exhortation: "in all things show yourself to be an example of good deeds, with purity in doctrine" (Titus 2:7).

REPROOF

"Reproof" points out what is sinful in our lives. The word refers to "the conviction of a sinner."5 In other words, Scripture accurately informs us exactly where we have gone wrong by helping us discern which choices have gotten us off God's good path of obedience. Peter uses a form of this word when referring to how God rebuked Balaam by using "a mute donkey, speaking with a voice of a man" (2 Peter 2:16). The psalmist also mentions the value of God's words to reprove us: "Moreover, by them Thy servant is warned; in keeping them there is great reward" (Ps. 19:11).

Biblical counselors must always remember that, when rebuke is necessary, there is no more effective tool than the Word of God. The Holy Spirit will use His own writings to make custom application to each disciple in a way that prompts repentance and fuels life-change. A serious example of reproof is the occasion when the Apostle Paul was forced to oppose Peter "to his face" because, by his hypocritical living, he was not being "straightforward about the truth of the gospel" (Gal. 2:11–14).

CORRECTION

The word translated "correction" means "setting up straight."6 God's Word not only convicts us and reproves us for our disobedience, but it also teaches us how to get back on the right track so that we can be useful vessels for the Master.

A biblical illustration demonstrating how the words of God are used in a corrective manner is the personal ministry that the prophet Nathan had to King David (2 Sam. 12:1–15). The text explains, "the LORD sent Nathan to David" for the purpose of reproving him for his adultery with Bathsheba and the murder of her husband. The Holy Spirit helped Nathan choose his words carefully and, in order to get to David's heart, he told a short story about a rich man who stole a poor man's solitary lamb. Once David's anger was kindled against the rich man's sin and a longing for justice was created in his heart, Nathan declared, "You are the man!" In response to this painful confrontation, David said to Nathan, "I have sinned against the LORD." Nathan was then responsible for outlining the natural consequences that would follow David to his grave. Thus we see how the words of God delivered to a fellow sinner brought forth the fruit of reproof—correction and repentance.

As biblical counselors, then, we are freed from the burden of creating our own standards of godliness. Instead, we are responsible for using the Scriptures to correct brothers or sisters in error and leading them to obey God's commands, which "are not burdensome" (1 John 5:3). All will benefit from following David's example in praying for the Spirit to use the Word to "Search me, O God, and know my heart; try me and know my anxious thoughts; and see if there be any hurtful way in me, and lead me in the everlasting way" (Ps. 139:23–24).

TRAINING

"Training" has to do with the education of believers with Scripture. Richard Trench says the following about the Greek word *paideia* in relation to *epanorthosis*, "correction":

> *Paideia* is one of those words to which Christianity gave a deeper meaning … For the Greek, *paideia* simply meant "education." But those who had learned that "foolishness is bound up in the heart" both "of a child" and of man and that "the rod of correction will drive it far from him" (Prov. 22:15) gave *paideia* an additional meaning. All effectual instruction for sinful mankind includes and implies chastening, or "correction," in which there must be *epanorthosis*. *Epanorthosis*, which occurs only once in the New Testament, is closely related to *paideia* in 2 Timothy 3:16.[7]

After briefly discussing the ancient uses of the word in philosophy and theology, Trench then goes on to say that Augustine defined it as "'instruction *through vexations*.' And this is the predominant meaning of *paideia*."[8] The Word of God corrects us in order to train us to be godly.

As biblical counselors, we must see to it that our teaching of the Word of God does not consist in merely imparting knowledge, but also trains disciples to live for God "in righteousness," which sometimes comes about painfully by correction "through vexations." This production of righteousness leads to peace: "And the work of righteousness will be peace, and the service of righteousness, quietness and confidence forever" (Isa. 32:17). That is, as the Word convicts and corrects us, it shapes new life patterns: habits that please God, in order that we may live according to His pleasure. Curtis Thomas writes of the need for biblical counseling to have this well-rounded approach: "Our counsel has both a corrective purpose and a training process. Admonition by itself can create serious relational problems. It is when we take the time to gently train others in the way of righteousness that we complete the God-ordained cycle."9

The ultimate purpose of the Word of God is that believers may be "adequate, equipped for every good work." The word translated "adequate" means "complete, capable, proficient."10 Trench states in *Synonyms of the New Testament*, "*Artios* refers not only to the presence of all the parts that are necessary for completeness but also to the further adaptation and aptitude of these parts for their designed purpose. Paul says that the man of God should be furnished with all that is necessary to carry out his appointed work (2 Tim. 3:17)."11 The Scriptures are adequate equipment for the work of teaching, reproving, correcting, and training—for the work of discipleship. As we faithfully use God's Word to counsel one another, we are "equipped for every good work." "Equipped" comes from *exartizo*. The only other time this word is used in the New Testament is when Paul and his companions' "days … were ended" in Tyre (Acts 21:5), after they had completed the purpose for which they sailed there. We can conclude, therefore, that God has breathed out His Word so that we might have His all-sufficient tool for the carrying out of the good work of discipling one another toward the purpose of becoming obedient followers of Jesus. Another significant demonstration of the sufficiency of Scripture is its power to perform surgery where true change begins—in the heart.

Surgery from the Word (Heb. 4:12)

Hebrews 4:12 begins with the little word "for." "*For* the word of God is living and active and sharper than any two-edged sword, and piercing as far as the division of soul and spirit, of both joints and marrow, and able to judge the thoughts and intentions of the heart." "For" is a connecting word that takes us back to the previous verses, where we learn of Jesus, the Living Word, who is our spiritual rest. In other words, by faith in His finished work on Calvary we enter our Sabbath, where we rest from the works of human achievement as the basis of acceptance with God. However, like the Israelites in the days of Moses and Joshua, we as believers must guard our hearts from a spirit of unbelief by remaining "diligent to enter that rest, so that no one will fall, through following the same example of disobedience" (v. 11). There is an accountability that comes to all who hear the Word of God as they did, and it is this powerful Word that the author now reminds his readers to heed.

These readers had heard enough of God's Word to know what He required of them, yet they remained on the edge of unbelief. If they failed to appropriate the spiritual rest found only in Christ, they would be in danger of becoming immune to the truth and, therefore, untouchable. This is as real a danger today as it was then. Anytime a person is confronted by the truth of God's Word, standing on the edge of belief, and fails to step over in faith, there is a risk of falling away from that place of sensitivity to the Spirit of God. The warning is very real. Thus Hebrews 4:12 presents the solution to this problem: submitting to the authority of Christ and the transforming power of Scripture. Here we are given five characteristics of the Word of God that further convince us of its sufficiency for the ministry of counseling.

DIVINE BOOK

First, the Bible is "the word of God." It is divine. Its very first words reveal God as One who speaks. He spoke the universe into existence (Gen. 1); He spoke to man in the garden (Gen. 2); He spoke to the fathers of His chosen nation (Gen. 12; 15; 31); and He spoke to that nation through His prophets. Ultimately, He spoke to the world through His Son, the divine speech in human form (John 1:1–14; Heb. 1:2). Finally, God has chosen to record the revelation of His Son in written form in the text of the Scriptures, the Word of God.

When resisting Satan's temptations, Jesus said, "It is written, 'Man shall not live on bread alone, but on every word that proceeds out of the mouth of God'" (Matt. 4:4). Second Peter 1:19–21 describes the process whereby God's words were recorded by men:

> So we have the prophetic word made more sure, to which you do well to pay attention as to a lamp shining in a dark place, until the day dawns and the morning star arises in your hearts. But know this first of all, that no prophecy of Scripture is a matter of one's own interpretation, for no prophecy was ever made by an act of human will, but men moved by the Holy Spirit spoke from God.

Because of its inspiration, Scripture, "the prophetic word," is inerrant and, therefore, more reliable than even the most enthralling spiritual experience, even the one Peter had on the Mount of Transfiguration (vv. 17–18). The Holy Spirit carried the minds of Scripture's writers along so that what they wrote was "from God." Those who pay attention to what the Scriptures teach "do well." Charles Spurgeon writes,

> If we doubt God's Word about one thing, we shall have small confidence in it upon another thing. Sincere faith in God must treat all God's Word alike; for the faith which accepts one word of God and rejects another is evidently not faith in God, but faith in our own judgment, faith in our own taste … Let us hold fast, tenaciously, doggedly, with a death grip, to the truth of the inspiration of God's Word … Everything in the railway service depends on the accuracy of the signals: when these are wrong, life will be sacrificed. On the road to heaven we need unerring signals, or the catastrophe will be far more terrible.[12]

What God thinks, He has spoken, and it is recorded for us in Scripture. Therefore, the Bible is the mind of God in written form and, as such, is completely authoritative.

Because the Bible is a divine book, it speaks with God's absolute authority. Consequently, one of the very first principles biblical counselors must establish is the authority of the Scriptures over everything that is thought, spoken, and believed by both counselors and counselees. Until counselees believe the Word enough to submit their hearts, minds, and wills to its authority, nothing of great value can be accomplished. As long as the opinions of counselees reign supreme, counselors cannot take them anywhere. Worst of all are the instances when counselees believe they have received a "personal" word from the Lord and use that to justify their attitudes and actions. Counselors will subsequently find that they cannot lead these people down the road of obedience. As Jonathan Edwards observes, "As long as a person has a notion that he is guided by immediate direction from heaven, it makes him incorrigible and impregnable in all his misconduct."[13]

LIVING BOOK

Second, the Bible is able to change the heart because it is alive. The word "living" is from the Greek verb meaning "to live."[14] It is in the present tense and could be translated, "constantly actively alive." Because it is the voice of Jesus Christ the Living Word, the Bible never rests. It is always working. A. W. Tozer says it well: "It is the present Voice which makes the written Word all-powerful. Otherwise it would lie locked in slumber within the covers of a book."[15] Being alive, it is also life-giving. It is able to save the soul. "Therefore, putting aside all filthiness and all that remains of wickedness, in humility receive the word implanted, which is able to save your souls" (James 1:21). Only a living book can give life to others. The prophet Jeremiah recognized this: "Your words were found and I ate them, and Your words became for me a joy and the delight of my heart" (15:16). The psalmist writes, "This is my comfort in my affliction, that Your word has revived me" (119:50).

Because the Bible is alive, it breathes forth God's power to save and to sanctify. Jesus prayed for His disciples, "Sanctify them in the truth; Your word is truth" (John 17:17). As biblical counselors, we must place our confidence in the ability of the Word of God, in the hands of the Spirit of God, to perform the work of God in conforming disciples to the image of Christ. In contrast, the behavioral theories of men are dead and, consequently, powerless to change hearts.

ACTIVE BOOK

Third, the Bible is productive. "Active" comes from the word from which we get "energy." It means to energize or be productive.[16] While the Bible is constantly actively alive, it is also productive. In other words, Scripture is God's instrument for the production of spiritual results. God promised this to Isaiah:

> For as the heavens are higher than the earth,
> So are My ways higher than your ways,
> And My thoughts than your thoughts.
> For as the rain and the snow come down from heaven,
> And do not return there without watering the earth,
> And making it bear and sprout,
> And furnishing seed to the sower and bread to the eater;
> So will My word be which goes forth from My mouth;
> It will not return to Me empty,

Without accomplishing what I desire,
And without succeeding in the matter for which I sent it.

55:9–11

When the spring rains feed the earth, the growth is obvious as buds begin to open and grass turns green. The same is true of the Bible: "so will My word be." Whenever the Word of God goes forth in the work of discipleship, it is like spiritual rain being poured out upon God's people and the result is growth and fruitfulness. In other words, God never sends His Word without accomplishing something for His glory.

Biblical counselors, therefore, must rest on this promised work, since change is not always immediately evident to us. However, this does not mean that the Spirit is not working in us or in those we are counseling. It takes time for fruit to become visible, but God's Word will change lives. We don't have to "doctor" it up to make it more appealing. We don't have to manipulate it. We just need to speak it in love and let it do its work because God has made an eternal covenant with His Word. He will always bless it with fruit.

PENETRATING BOOK

Fourth, the Bible is a piercing book. The adjective "sharper" originates from the primitive root *temno*, meaning, "to cut."[17] The Word has cutting power. In other words, the Word of God is incisively penetrating. As a two-edged sword pierces through body parts, so the Word of God pierces through the innermost man. It does not go just into the head, but it pierces the deepest parts of the inner being. It may shape our thoughts without at first our realizing that we are changing, which then brings our minds closer to God's way of thinking. John Calvin says, "If anyone thinks that the air is beaten by an empty sound when the Word of God is preached, he is greatly mistaken; for it is a living thing and full of hidden power, which leaves nothing in man untouched."[18] The Word of God is not stagnant. When confronted by its truth, we are always forced to make a decision. It will not let anyone remain neutral.

A biblical illustration of the penetrating power of the Word is found in the book of Acts. On the day of Pentecost, Peter preached a message of which the main point was, "Men of Judea, throughout biblical history God promised to send you a Messiah, and when He came, you killed Him."

When they heard him say, "whom *you* crucified" (2:36), his hearers knew exactly what he meant. At that point, the truth hit them between the eyes and they realized what they had done to Jesus. The next verse says, "Now when they heard this, they were pierced to the heart." The two-edged sword of the Word of God demanded a response from its hearers—"what shall we do?" The answer was, "Repent" (2:38). The piercing Word twists and turns to expose whatever is in our hearts that must be repented of. It is the divine scalpel used by the Divine Surgeon to cut and expose the cancerous sin that must be dealt with in order to gain spiritual health.

Biblical counselors, therefore, must let the Word of God do its cutting work. We must always speak the truth in love, but we must always speak the truth. Our counseling must be Word-saturated so that the Spirit's tool will be readily available for Him to convict those in sin and bring them to repentance. But we must also be careful to remember that God does not overwhelm His children by showing us all our sinful ways at once. Believers are His works in progress (Phil. 1:6), and His ways are filled with compassion and grace (Ps. 103:8).

DISCERNING BOOK

Fifth and finally, the Bible is a discerning book. The Word is able to "judge," "to discern."[19] The Greek word is *kritikos*, from which we get "critical." This is the only occurrence of this adjective, but the root *kritays* is used throughout the New Testament of God as Judge and of men when they act like judges (e.g. Heb. 12:23; James 4:11). The Scripture is able to analyze and sift out the deepest portions of our inner being, "the thoughts and intentions of the heart." In other words, it weighs out the reflections of our minds and the affections of our hearts in order to show us right from wrong. God said, "I, the LORD, search the heart, I test the mind" (Jer. 17:10). He does this through His Word. "The unfolding of Your words gives light; it gives understanding to the simple" (Ps. 119:130).

Biblical counselors, then, must use the "sword of the Spirit" (Eph. 6:17), the Word of God, for the "destruction of fortresses" and the taking of "every thought captive to the obedience of Christ" (2 Cor. 10:4–5). The fortresses Paul is speaking of are the false ways of thinking and the philosophies of the world. Knowing the Word enables us to take those foolish speculations and conform them to the Word, which automatically results in thoughts that are obedient to Christ. A. W. Pink correctly notes, "There is only one safeguard against error, and that is to be established in the faith; and for that, there has to be prayerful and diligent study, and a receiving with meekness the engrafted Word of God."[20] As we faithfully employ the Scriptures in counseling, we will train disciples to discern the wrong ways of thinking that have become fortresses for sin in their lives, so that their minds can be renewed and their lives transformed.

Scripture memorization

In light of the sufficiency of the Word of God and its ability to perform the heart surgery required for spiritual health, biblical counselors would be wise to make memorizing Scripture a standard homework assignment for those they are discipling. In his book *Transforming Grace*, Jerry Bridges convinces us of the relationship of Bible intake to spiritual growth:

> It is not enough to only hear it preached or taught in our churches on Sundays, as important as those avenues are. We need a regular plan of reading, study, and yes, even memorization. Bible study and Scripture memorization earn no merit with God. We never earn God's blessing by doing these things, anymore than we earn His blessing by eating nutritious food. But as the eating of proper food is necessary to sustain a healthy physical life, so the regular intake of God's word is necessary to sustain a healthy spiritual life and to regularly appropriate God's grace.[21]

There are at least four practical benefits received from the regular intake of God's Word through the discipline of Scripture memory.

IT FEEDS BIBLICAL MEDITATION

First, the chief purpose of memorizing Scripture is to promote biblical meditation. Meditation takes the memorizing of biblical texts to the deeper level of transforming one's inner being, which will then lead to change of character. The common disconnect between practical godliness and Bible knowledge that was addressed in the fourth chapter of this book highlights the importance of meditation. The pews of churches today are often filled with people who have won awards for Bible memory, but who have not internalized the Scriptures by meditating on the knowledge they have acquired. Scripture memorization is not to be done merely for a reward or to gain knowledge for knowledge's sake, but God's Word makes it clear that

He richly blesses those who continually muse on His Word, which results in spiritual stability and fruitfulness.

> How blessed is the man who does not walk in the counsel of the wicked,
>   Nor stand in the path of sinners,
>   Nor sit in the seat of scoffers!
> But his delight is in the law of the LORD,
>   And in His law he meditates day and night.
> He will be like a tree firmly planted by streams of water,
>   Which yields its fruit in its season,
>   And its leaf does not wither;
>   And in whatever he does, he prospers.
>
> Ps. 1:1–3

In addition to increasing spiritual strength and causing fruitfulness to burst forth, Scripture meditation should lead to habitual obedience to God, which results in success:

> This book of the law shall not depart from your mouth, but you shall meditate on it day and night, so that you may be careful to do according to all that is written in it; for then you will make your way prosperous, and then you will have success. Have I not commanded you? Be strong and courageous! Do not tremble or be dismayed, for the LORD your God is with you wherever you go.
>
> Josh. 1:8–9

To "meditate" means to ponder, to think deeply upon a particular biblical truth. The Hebrew word used in both Psalm 1:2 and Joshua 1:8 carries the idea of speaking to oneself. *Strong's Exhaustive Concordance* says that, in addition to "ponder," the word also means to "moan, growl, utter, [and] speak."[22] Biblical meditation, therefore, is the practice of purposely mulling God's truth over and over in our minds throughout the day until it grips our hearts and changes us within. John Quincy Adams, while lamenting to his son about his own lack of discipline in meditating on the Scriptures, writes,

> Even meditation itself is often fruitless, unless it has some special object in view; useful thoughts often arise in the mind, and pass away without being remembered or applied to any good purpose—like the seed scattered upon the surface of the ground, which the birds devour, or the wind blows away, or

which rot without taking root, however good the soil may be upon which they are cast.[23]

Meditation toward the goal of pleasing God firmly plants His truth within us so that we may be continually conformed to the image of Christ. It accomplishes this by renewing our thought patterns, transforming our desires, directing our emotions, and moving our will in the direction of godliness.

One good way to make sure that God's Word is readily available to meditate on day and night is to memorize it, which, in turn, guides our thoughts, which then determine our words and actions, which ultimately result in success in God's eyes. The psalmist prayed, "Let the words of my mouth and the meditation of my heart be acceptable in Your sight, O Lord, my rock and my Redeemer" (Ps. 19:14). One way to ensure that our words and thoughts are pleasing to God is by regularly stuffing our minds with truth through Scripture memorization.

It flushes the mind of sinful thought patterns

Second, memorizing Scripture is often God's means of hitting sin's bull's-eye. I know of no more effective means of attacking a particular sin in our lives than selecting from the Word of God specific truths that can function as arrows to be directed at the heart problems behind our sinful habits. As we repent of (put off) sin and replace it with (put on) righteousness, we must at the same time renew our minds with truth that will change the intentions of our hearts to be pleasing to God. This is what Paul taught the believers in the cities of Ephesus and Rome:

> … that, in reference to your former manner of life, you lay aside the old self, which is being corrupted in accordance with the lusts of deceit, and that you *be renewed in the spirit of your mind*, and put on the new self, which in the likeness of God has been created in righteousness and holiness of the truth.
>
> Eph. 4:22–24

> Therefore I urge you, brethren, by the mercies of God, to present your bodies a living and holy sacrifice, acceptable to God, which is your spiritual service of worship. And do not be conformed to this world, but *be transformed by the*

renewing of your mind, so that you may prove what the will of God is, that which is good and acceptable and perfect.

Rom. 12:1–2

Notice how the believer's life is transformed by replacing worldly thought patterns with godly ones. As we fill our minds with the fresh, clear water of the Word, it forces out the dirty, brown water of the world, which results in the fulfillment of the will of God. If we want to help our counselees find and fulfill God's will for their lives, encouraging them to memorize Scripture will surely be taking a step in the right direction.

IT FORCES OUR EMOTIONS TO SUBMIT

Third, memorizing Scripture helps train our emotions to submit to God. Psalm 42 is one example of this. This psalm is a wonderful song of testimony to God as the Helper of those in despair. Throughout the poem, we notice the man's low emotional state by descriptive phrases such as "My tears have been my food" (v. 3) and "Why are you in despair, O my soul?" (vv. 5, 11). He tells us that he poured out his soul as he remembered a previous time when he was closer to the Lord (v. 4). As his critics became more vocal, he cried out to God, "Why have You forgotten me?" (v. 9). It is obvious that this man was struggling with spiritual depression. But how did he deal with it?

The answer is that he worked through the depression by talking to himself through reciting biblical truth about what God is like. He reminded himself that God is "the living God," and about "the help of His presence" and the way He commands His "lovingkindness in the daytime" (vv. 2, 5, 8). Twice he told himself to "Hope in God," being confident that "I shall yet praise Him" (vv. 5, 11). In other words, he fought off his unreliable feelings with what he knew to be true of God. Martyn Lloyd-Jones explains the difference between talking to ourselves and letting "ourselves" talk to us. In his book *Spiritual Depression: Its Causes and Cure*, he writes,

> How do we reconcile the two things? In this way. I say that we must talk to ourselves instead of allowing "ourselves" to talk to us! Do you realize what that means? I suggest that the main trouble in this whole matter of spiritual depression in a sense is this, that we allow our self to talk to us instead of talking to our self. Am I just trying to be deliberately paradoxical? Far from it. This is the very essence of wisdom in this matter. Have you realized that most of your unhappiness in life is due to the fact that you are listening to yourself

instead of talking to yourself? Take those thoughts that come to you the moment you wake up in the morning. You have not originated them, but they start talking to you, they bring back the problems of yesterday, etc. Somebody is talking. Who is talking to you? Your self is talking to you. Now this man's treatment [in Ps. 42] was this; instead of allowing this self to talk to him, he starts talking to himself. "Why art thou cast down, O my soul?" he asks. His soul had been depressing him, crushing him. So he stands up and says: "Self, listen for a moment, I will speak to you" … The main art in the matter of spiritual living is to know how to handle yourself. You have to take yourself in hand, you have to address yourself, preach to yourself, question yourself.[24]

What Lloyd-Jones was essentially saying is that we must renew our minds with God's truth. We must demand that our feelings fall into line with God's Word. We must use Scripture to whip our emotions into shape. We must flush out self-focus and self-pity with the fresh water of hope in God. One simple way to feed this habit is by memorizing Scripture.

It fortifies the will to choose God's way

Fourth, we prepare for temptation by memorizing what Scripture says about the sinful habits we war against. One of the very first verses I memorized as a brand-new believer is 1 Corinthians 10:13: "No temptation has overtaken you but such as is common to man; and God is faithful, who will not allow you to be tempted beyond what you are able, but with the temptation will provide the way of escape also, so that you will be able to endure it." This verse helped me greatly in those infantile years of my faith, and still helps me today, since temptation can come at any time, especially when we least expect it.

The psalmist testified, "Your word I have treasured in my heart that I may not sin against You" (Ps. 119:11). Apparently he knew that the more Scripture he treasured within his heart (no doubt at least partly by memory), the less he would sin. In other words, he believed that valuing God's Word enough to store it up in his heart would protect him from evil. Donald Whitney testifies, "A pertinent scriptural truth, brought to your awareness by the Holy Spirit at just the right moment, can be the weapon that makes the difference in a spiritual battle."[25]

Probably the best illustration of how Scripture memory strengthens the will to resist temptation is Jesus' response to the devil's attacks. Three times, in Matthew 4:1–11, our Lord quoted Scripture word for word to Satan, and His use of Bible verses was like firing specific arrows at specific targets (vv. 4, 7, 10). For instance, when the devil tempted him to turn stones into bread, Jesus quoted a verse about the sufficiency of God's bread, the Word of God. When Satan tempted Jesus to throw Himself down to the ground, He recited a verse about not putting God's promise of protection to the test. And when the devil tempted Jesus to gain all things through false worship, Jesus quoted verses about true worship that surrenders to God alone.

Scripture memory is an indispensable tool in the disciple-making process because transformation of life begins in the mind and heart. Long before sin shows its ugly head in visible forms, our flesh has been indulging itself in its thoughts (Eph. 2:3). Consequently, we must "be renewed in the spirit of [our] mind" (Eph. 4:23) by submitting every thought to the authority of the Word of God.

Summary

The church of the living God is "the pillar and support of the truth" (1 Tim. 3:15). Clearly, it is the church's responsibility to uphold the truth of God as revealed in His Word. Therefore, when a church forsakes the sufficiency of Scripture and commits adultery with psychological counseling, it fails to live up to its calling to defend the truth of God in a world of man-centered theory. However, not only does an unfaithful church thereby fail in its witness for God in the world, but it also commits spiritual suicide by pulling the plug on its own life-support system. Eventually its internal organs begin to shut down and the individual parts of the body cease to thrive. There can be no spiritual health without spiritual food, and there is no food as pure as the bread of the Word that "proceeds out of the mouth of God" (Matt. 4:4).

What is needed today is a godly audacity to hold to the absolute sufficiency of Scripture, to believe that man can really become completely new in Jesus Christ without the aid of psychological manipulation, mood-altering drugs, or self-help theories, and to believe that the very breath of the living God can and will transform sinners from the inside out. This is the very purpose for which the Scriptures were given: to teach, reprove, correct, and train us to live Christ-centered lives so that we may become complete in Him.

This divine book, the mind of God in written form, actively produces fruit in the lives of those who humbly submit to its living authority. It penetrates to the innermost parts of our being—convicting us of sin and forcing us to choose between pleasing God or pleasing self. As such, it stands supreme over all other books. In the book *Gospel Fear*, Jeremiah Burroughs writes,

> Nothing in the world has authority over men's consciences but the Word of the Lord, and that has authority. It has authority to bind consciences, to awe and terrify men. So a gracious heart sees the great seal of heaven stamped upon every truth in God's Word and, therefore, dares not trifle with it as it did before. It comes to the Word either as to a sovereign to receive laws, or as to a judge to receive the sentence of condemnation. That soul now looks upon the Word as backed with such authority that either it must yield unto it or else it binds that soul over to eternal death by such bonds that all the power of all creatures in heaven and earth cannot loose it again.[26]

This is the tool that the Holy Spirit has left for us to use in cooperation with Him in the process of making obedient followers of Jesus Christ. It is time to unleash the Sword of the living God through the ministry of targeted discipleship. And it is time to go to war against the ungodly philosophies of men.

For further thought and small-group discussion

1. Read Psalm 19:7–9. Discuss the immeasurable value of the Word of God and the work it performs in our hearts and minds.

2. Read 2 Timothy 3:16–17. Discuss the meaning of the words:

- profitable
- teaching
- reproof
- correction
- training
- equipped.

3. Read Hebrews 4:12. Discuss the power of the Word of God to perform surgery on our hearts.

4. Read Psalm 1:1–3. Discuss the benefits of meditating on Scripture. How does memorizing Scripture aid meditation? Do you have a plan for regular Scripture memorization? If not, will you make one this week?

5. Read Psalm 42. Discuss how the psalmist used biblical truth to talk himself out of depression. Make a list of biblical truths about God that will help you change your focus the next time you are depressed.

The combat against worldly psychology

Chapter 7

For I am jealous for you with a godly jealousy; for I betrothed you to one husband, so that to Christ I might present you as a pure virgin. But I am afraid that, as the serpent deceived Eve by his craftiness, your minds will be led astray from the simplicity and purity of devotion to Christ.

–2 Cor. 11:2–3

For though we walk in the flesh, we do not war according to the flesh, for the weapons of our warfare are not of the flesh, but divinely powerful for the destruction of fortresses. We are destroying speculations and every lofty thing raised up against the knowledge of God, and we are taking every thought captive to the obedience of Christ, and we are ready to punish all disobedience, whenever your obedience is complete.

–2 Cor. 10:3–6

Authentic biblical counseling grips the wisdom of God embodied and revealed in Jesus Christ and refuses to surrender the higher ground of the Holy Spirit's revelation of Truth in the gospel to the inferior wisdom of man. God's vision of discipleship requires that disciple-makers be unafraid of waging war against the prevailing anti-Christian or sub-Christian philosophies that diminish Jesus Christ and strip His gospel of the offense of the cross and, consequently, limit its power to transform lives. Therefore, we must resist the integration of worldly psychology into Christian theology, which conceals Christ and undermines faith in the sufficiency of the Word of God for life and godliness. Thus, Christian psychology must be viewed for what it is: another gospel, a subtle tool of the enemy to lure believers away from pure devotion to Jesus Christ.

God's wisdom challenged

It was this same mixture of human wisdom and the gospel that deceived followers of Christ and broke the Apostle Paul's heart. As a result, he was compelled to write another letter to the church at Corinth. Paul had a tender relationship with the believers there, since he had planted the church through eighteen months of teaching the Word (Acts 18:11). Later, when he heard of numerous problems among them, including divisions, immoralities, lawsuits, abuses of the Lord's Supper, and many other distresses, he wrote the corrective letter we know as First Corinthians. Soon even more disturbing news reached Paul's ears. Self-proclaimed apostles were taking over the church by attacking his character. They openly insulted him by saying that he was ugly, he was not a dynamic public speaker, and that his physical stature was unimpressive. In Paul's mind, all of these accusations were true and, therefore, were not very bothersome to him. However, when he heard that his disciples were being led away from Christ-centered devotion, that was a different story. The jealousy of his pastoral heart was fiercely set in motion.

This beloved teacher confessed, "For I am jealous for you with a godly jealousy; for I betrothed you to one husband, so that to Christ I might present you as a pure virgin. But I am afraid that, as the serpent deceived Eve by his craftiness, your minds will be led astray from the simplicity and purity of devotion to Christ" (2 Cor. 11:2–3). Paul was grieved to learn of how they were subtly directed away from Christ into an adulterous relationship with human wisdom. It was their "minds" that had been deceived. Satan was at work, and the result was a departure from the sufficiency of Christ and His inerrant Word. The same problem exists today.

In his book *A Biblical Theology of the Church*, Mal Couch comments on the modern drift away from the Word of God as the chief means by which counselors minister to the spiritual needs of God's people:

> Some would argue that in modern times the approach to pastoral care should be different from the past. It is true that certain practices and methods can be replaced, but the substance of pastoral care is the same. And the source must be the same—the Word of God. But many are drifting from this and substituting psychology for biblical and spiritual comfort.[1]

A remarkable testimony to the inspiration of the Scriptures is their relevance to the concerns of the day, no matter what age we live in. Christians living today may think that an attempt to integrate man's wisdom, which is "earthly, natural, demonic" (James 3:15), with the truth of

God's Word is something relatively new, but nothing could be further from the truth. In fact, the Apostle Paul confronted this same problem in the first-century church at Corinth.

Not far into his first letter, the apostle exalted the gospel of Jesus Christ above worldly wisdom. In fact, he specifically warned the church of the natural human tendency to conceal Christ through "cleverness of speech" (1 Cor. 1:17). This should have hit home to the Corinthians since they thought the world of worldly wisdom. What was unclear to them was obvious to Paul—that the chief cause of the divisions they suffered was their confidence in their own wisdom, which would only lead to "jealousy and selfish ambition … disorder and every evil thing" (James 3:16). However, God's wisdom "is first pure, then peaceable, gentle, reasonable, full of mercy and good fruits, unwavering, without hypocrisy" (James 3:17).

The apostle rightly viewed human philosophy as a subtle attack on the biblical gospel. Consequently, Paul engaged in active combat against the invasion of worldly wisdom into the church in order that "the cross of Christ would not be made void" (1 Cor. 1:17b). "Made void" means "to dwindle to nothing, to vanish under the weight of rhetorical ornament."[2] Charles Hodge states it well: "whatever obscures the cross deprives the Gospel of its power."[3] Paul's point was that the gospel loses its power when it is cloaked in worldly wisdom.

The wisdom of worldly psychology does not bring people closer to God, but turns faith inward and thereby leads them away from the hope and the power of God's salvation found outside themselves—in Jesus Christ. Don Matzat, in his book *Christ Esteem*, writes, "While humanistic psychology teaches us to know ourselves so that we might feel good about ourselves, biblical Christianity teaches us to know ourselves so that we might turn away from ourselves and discover our life and identity in Christ Jesus."[4] As the wisdom of God personified, Jesus Christ is the center of God's revelation, and His wisdom is superior to anything man-centered psychology has to offer.

In the first two chapters of 1 Corinthians, the Apostle Paul launches three massive counter-attacks on integrationism. First, he demonstrates the superiority of God's revelation in Christ over the wisdom of man. Second, he argues that the wisdom of God is gloriously displayed in the gospel.

Third, he explains the indispensable work of the Holy Spirit in revealing the wisdom of God to the mind of man.

GOD'S WISDOM SUPERIOR TO HUMAN PHILOSOPHY (1 COR. 1:18–25)

> For the word of the cross is foolishness to those who are perishing, but to us who are being saved it is the power of God. For it is written, "I will destroy the wisdom of the wise, and the cleverness of the clever I will set aside." Where is the wise man? Where is the scribe? Where is the debater of this age? Has not God made foolish the wisdom of the world? For since in the wisdom of God the world through its wisdom did not come to know God, God was well-pleased through the foolishness of the message preached to save those who believe. For indeed Jews ask for signs and Greeks search for wisdom; but we preach Christ crucified, to Jews a stumbling block and to Gentiles foolishness, but to those who are the called, both Jews and Greeks, Christ the power of God and the wisdom of God. Because the foolishness of God is wiser than men, and the weakness of God is stronger than men.

Since he has already established the preaching of Christ as his highest priority (1 Cor. 1:17), the apostle continues to turn the Corinthians' attention away from humanistic philosophy to "the word of the cross." In verse 17, he mentions the cleverness of words, the *logos* of speech, which hides the gospel from man. However, in verse 18, he refers to the *logos* of the cross, the word of the crucified Christ. In other words, he is exalting the wisdom of Christ over the foolishness of men. This is seen in the repetitive use of the words "foolishness" or "fool" (five times), and "wisdom" or "wise" (nine times). This contrast between God's wisdom in Christ and the foolishness of human philosophy highlights six elements of God's revelation that establish its superiority.

The priority of God's revelation

First, the revelation of God in Christ is superior to the wisdom of men because it is the only message that has the power to redeem sinners. The phrase "the word of the cross" (v. 18) refers to the whole doctrine of Christ and His all-sufficient work of salvation. The cross proclaims God's righteousness, being the culmination of a just God breaking into time to purchase unjust sinners (Rom. 3:25–26). Christ bore in His body the penalty that we deserve (1 Peter 2:24), was victorious over sin and Satan (Heb. 2:14), propitiated the wrath of God (1 John 4:10), and opened the floodgate of God's mercy upon sinners (Eph. 2:4–5).

Though the message of the cross is God's greatest statement of grace and the only hope for depraved sinners, it seems foolish "to those who are perishing." The word "perishing" comes from a very strong word that means "to destroy."[5] It is in the present tense, which indicates that unbelievers are not only lost, but are presently in the process of being ruined. This reinforces the fact that what is required to rescue hell-bound sinners out of a state of perpetual death is not a psychological gospel that persuades them to think more highly of themselves, but rather a supernatural work of God outside themselves—the whole gospel of Jesus Christ.

Unless enlightened by the Holy Spirit, the unbeliever sliding down a slippery slope toward hell considers the word of the cross "foolishness." This word comes from *moria*, from which we get "moron." The gospel is nonsense to unregenerate sinners because it exposes their inability to save themselves and is, therefore, contrary to human wisdom. Gordon Fee writes, "No mere human, in his or her right mind or otherwise, would ever have dreamed up God's scheme for redemption—through a crucified Messiah. It is too preposterous, too humiliating, for a God."[6] Consequently, sinners who refuse to acknowledge their sinfulness ultimately think of the cross as an unnecessary joke. Until unbelievers sees themselves as sinners worthy of the same death that Jesus endured, the message of Christ will continue to sound ridiculous to them. As long as they continue to believe the message of the psychological gospel—that they are wounded and needy victims rather than idolatrous sinners—they will not be driven to Christ, the only One who can truly set them free (John 8:36). But, while it is foolishness to the unbeliever, the cross is "the power of God" to the believer in Jesus Christ.

The permanency of God's revelation
Second, the endurance of God's revelation is set in contrast to the destruction of human wisdom. Man's wisdom will be destroyed, but the truth of God in Christ will endure forever, "For it is written, 'I will destroy the wisdom of the wise, and the cleverness of the clever I will set aside'" (1:19). The phrase "set aside" means "to do away with."[7] Verse 19 is a loose quotation of Isaiah 29:14, which reminds us that the rebellious nation of Judah was about to be attacked by Sennacherib, king of Assyria. However, through

this prophecy, God assured Isaiah that the enemy's plan would fail, not because of the strength of Judah's army, but solely because of the power of God. In other words, God would destroy the enemy and manifest His might without human assistance. As a result, God sent one of His angels to destroy 185,000 Assyrian soldiers without using one ounce of human strength. So Paul asks, "Where is the wise man? Where is the scribe? Where is the debater of this age?" In other words, the worldly philosopher is nothing. Christ is everything! Thus, "God made foolish" the wisdom of the world (v. 20).

Man's wisdom cannot bring us to God because it is temporary, but the wisdom of God is eternal. Peter testifies the same: "'All flesh is like grass, and all its glory like the flower of grass. The grass withers, and the flower falls off, but the word of the LORD abides forever.' And this is the word which was preached to you" (1 Peter 1:24–25). Though the philosophies of the world will one day be destroyed and the theories of one psychologist will be replaced by those of the next, there is one thing that will remain the same: the Word of God. Jesus had full confidence in God's written revelation: "For truly I say to you, until heaven and earth pass away, not the smallest letter or stroke shall pass away from the Law until all is accomplished" (Matt. 5:18). The Bible forever stands against the blatant and subtle attacks of Satan's emissaries. It has endured the test of time, and will continue to do so.

The plan of God's revelation
Third, it is according to "the wisdom of God" that man is unable to find salvation through his own wisdom. This was God's sovereign plan from eternity past. Our wisdom is intentionally limited, for "the world through its wisdom did not come to know God" (v. 21a). The limitations of earthly wisdom explain how astronomers can study the order of the universe and still walk away believing that it all came from a spontaneous big bang. This is why scientists can examine the renewing capabilities of the human cell and still believe primordial man crawled out of a slime pit billions of years ago. This is why psychologists can research the behavior of man and not arrive at the conclusion that his greatest need is the spiritual rebirth and transformation that only God can perform by means of the gospel. The wisdom of man is foolishness to God, and the wisdom of God is foolishness to unregenerate man, revealing that, the more that man tries to find God through his own wisdom, the more he worships the creature rather than

the Creator. Subsequently, the more that the church seeks solutions to behavioral problems by integrating theology with psychology, the farther we drift from the God of truth.

The pleasure of God's revelation

Fourth, the revelation of God in Christ is superior to man's wisdom because it exalts His sovereign pleasure. Paul wrote, "God was well-pleased through the foolishness of the message preached to save those who believe" (1:21*b*). He is not saying that preaching itself is foolish, but that the content of the message is foolish to the mind that has not been renewed by the Spirit of God through the Word of God. According to William MacDonald, "The Greeks were lovers of wisdom (the literal meaning of the word 'philosophers'). But there was nothing in the gospel message to appeal to their pride of knowledge."[8] Therefore, it pleased God to save sinners in a way that man would never have dreamed of. The gospel may be foolish to man because it slaughters his pride, but it is not foolish to God. The cross says to man, "Never in all your days, not even if you possessed ten million lives, could you take care of your sin problem." However, the Christ who at one time hung on the cross saves "those who believe." He gives them spiritual life. In other words, it pleases God greatly to use the message of the cross to save those who cling to Jesus Christ for salvation through faith alone.

The preaching of God's revelation

The fifth element of God's revelation is its preaching, which focuses on "Christ crucified" (v. 23). However, Paul identifies two obstacles to spreading the message of the cross: a search for signs and rational explanations. The Jews of Jesus' day were always looking for a sign or a demonstration of His power because they would not take Him at His Word. Matthew 12:38–39 says, "Then some of the scribes and Pharisees said to Him, 'Teacher, we want to see a sign from You.' But He answered and said to them, 'An evil and adulterous generation craves for a sign; and yet no sign will be given to it but the sign of Jonah the prophet.'" Asking for signs is not a demonstration of faith, but a lack of submissive trust in God's revelation in Scripture. Therefore, to the Jew waiting for a miraculous sign, the message of a crucified Messiah was a "stumbling block" (*skandalon*); it was scandalous. Second, "Greeks search for wisdom" (v. 22). While the Jews looked for signs, the Greeks searched for rational explanations. They believed only that which could be understood and explained by human intelligence. To them, the preaching of the cross was foolish, ridiculous, insane, and sheer madness. Both of these kinds of people exist in churches today, largely because, in this therapeutic age, "preaching is psychologized."9

Similarly, the preaching of worldly psychology has trained a whole generation of believers to live by their feelings and experiences, always looking for some sign from God to confirm their subjective leadings, even though He has already clearly spelled out His will in His objective Word. Others gobble up the latest psychological theories in their never-ending quests for truth outside God's revelation. For both, faith in the crucified Christ is ultimately hijacked by human wisdom.

The power of God's revelation
Sixth and finally, the superiority of God's revelation is demonstrated by its inherent power. To the "called," the message of Christ is "the power of God and the wisdom of God" (v. 24). The "called" are God's elect, those who have received the outer call of the gospel through the preaching of the Word because of the inner effectual call of the Holy Spirit. Paul refers to the believers at Rome as "the called of Jesus Christ" (Rom. 1:6). Those "whom He predestined, He also called; and these whom He called, He also justified; and these whom He justified, He also glorified" (Rom. 8:30). As a result of the call of God, believers are regenerate, "born again not of seed which is perishable [like psychology] but imperishable, that is, through the living and enduring word of God" (1 Peter 1:23). Christ is "the power of God" because He rescues man from his fundamental problem—sin. Christ is also "the wisdom of God" because all eternal truth is revealed in Him.

Therefore, "the foolishness of God is wiser than men, and the weakness of God is stronger than men" (v. 25). The supposed foolishness of God, the cross, is still wiser than the wisdom of the wisest man. The weakness of God, if there ever were such a thing, is still stronger than the strongest man. What is the apostle's point? His point is that the power of God dwells in the gospel—the word of the cross. When the gospel is preached, the power of God is unleashed to accomplish what He has ordained—to convict sinners and draw them to repentance. Therefore, we affirm, "For I am not ashamed of the gospel, for it is the power of God for salvation to everyone who believes, to the Jew first and also to the Greek" (Rom. 1:16).

The revelation of God in Christ is radically distinct from anything the world of psychological counseling can offer. By its very nature, worldly psychology is antagonistic to the cross. As it exalts man's wisdom, it diminishes Jesus Christ, the very source of truth (John 14:6). David Powlison testifies, "After years in the psychotherapeutic world, I found that Christ turned my life upside down. Then I started to see that he turned the whole world upside down: *everything* was God-centered, not man-centered. That meant that counseling needed a fundamental realignment to inhabit the real world, not the world fabricated by unbelief."[10] To attempt to integrate biblical theology with psychology is, therefore, utterly foolish and will only lead to the exaltation of man, which in turn leads to his spiritual ruin.

GOD'S WISDOM DISPLAYED IN THE GOSPEL **(1 COR. 2:6–9)**

> Yet we do speak wisdom among those who are mature; a wisdom, however, not of this age, nor of the rulers of this age, who are passing away; but we speak God's wisdom in a mystery, the hidden wisdom which God predestined before the ages to our glory; the wisdom which none of the rulers of this age has understood; for if they had understood it, they would not have crucified the Lord of glory; but just as it is written, "Things which eye has not seen and ear has not heard, and which have not entered the heart of man, all that God has prepared for those who love Him."

We have already seen that the wisdom of God revolves around one basic message—Jesus Christ, crucified for sinners and risen from the dead to give spiritual life to those who believe. So, as the Apostle Paul continues to use the word "wisdom" in reference to true wisdom, what needs to come to our minds is the gospel, which he describes in six ways.

The gospel is true wisdom
First, in contrast to those who believed that the apostles had nothing worthwhile to say, Paul declared, "we do speak wisdom" (v. 6*a*). That is, we speak the revelation of God in Christ to the "mature," those who have been "initiated"[11] into fellowship with Christ by faith. Paul is not offering theology as an add-on to worldly wisdom; but rather is keeping the two in their separate spheres. He is not distinguishing between two classes of

Christians, but between believers and unbelievers, the enlightened and the unenlightened. In our day, as in Paul's, those who elevate worldly psychology above God's Word consider themselves to be the enlightened ones, and we who stand solely on the Scriptures, the archaic, unenlightened ones. However, Scripture declares the opposite. Jay Adams rightly asserts,

> God has revealed much truth in the Bible, and we dare not open our thinking (let alone our practice) to any theories or practices that prove to be out of accord with biblical teaching. Unfortunately, not too many persons—especially in the field of counseling—operate according to that presupposition. But, I insist, if we are to make headway in Christian thought in any area of life, we must agree not only that whatever God says in the Bible is true and authoritative, but also that because of this fact our minds must remain closed to anything that contradicts, attempts to supplant, or otherwise interferes with biblical principles and practices. If, operationally, Christian counselors would only adhere to this critical presupposition, they would save themselves much confusion and heartache and would realize more of God's blessing on their work.[12]

Those who trust God's revelation in Christ and accept it as ultimate truth are the ones who possess true wisdom and, therefore, have a divine obligation to keep it unstained by every idea that is false.

The gospel is not of this age
Second, Paul speaks of a wisdom that is "not of this age" (v. 6b). When he declared that he did indeed possess wisdom, the Corinthians may have immediately thought of the worldly philosophies of their day. So he makes it clear that that is not what he is writing about. In Christ, he possesses a wisdom that is unlike anything human. Simon Kistemaker writes, "The wisdom of this age is identical with worldly wisdom (1:20) that is characterized by a fleeting and changeable nature."[13] As Psalm 94:11 says, "The LORD knows the thoughts of man, that they are a mere breath." Though the theories of worldly psychology are constantly changing, the wisdom of God in the gospel is inflexible because it is rooted in Jesus Christ, who is "the same yesterday and today and forever" (Heb. 13:8).

The gospel is hidden from temporal rulers
Third, God's wisdom does not come from the "rulers" of this age (v. 6b). In

fact, it is hidden from "the great men of authority."[14] The great philosophers of our day are not the storehouses of God's truth even though that may be what they arrogantly assert. One can only imagine that if Job were alive today, he would sarcastically say to many psychologists, "Truly then you are the people, and with you wisdom will die!" (Job 12:2). Instead of entrusting His wisdom to those who reject Him, God keeps His wisdom hidden from the intellectual elite so that He retains the glory that rightly belongs to Him alone.

Later, when referring to unbelieving Jews, the apostle argues that God kept His wisdom hidden behind a veil, because "their minds were hardened; for until this very day at the reading of the old covenant the same *veil* remains unlifted, because it is removed in Christ. But to this day whenever Moses is read, a *veil* lies over their heart; but whenever a person turns to the Lord, the *veil* is taken away" (2 Cor. 3:14–16). In the same way, the wisdom of God is hidden from some because of unbelief. The rulers of our age are "passing away," meaning that they are being "put out of commission."[15] God is removing power and influence from earthly leaders who do not exalt His wisdom embodied in His glorious Son. In fact, "He who sits in the heavens laughs, the Lord scoffs at them" (Ps. 2:4).

The gospel is now revealed to some people

Fourth, though God's wisdom is hidden from the worldly-wise, it is revealed to some. Jesus said the same: "I praise You, Father, Lord of heaven and earth, that You have hidden these things from the wise and intelligent and have revealed them to infants" (Matt. 11:25). This is what Paul means by "we speak God's wisdom in a mystery" (v. 7a). G. Campbell Morgan wrote, "A mystery in the New Testament always means something undiscoverable by the activity of the human intellect, but revealed, so that human intellect can understand."[16] That mystery is the truth of redemption found only in Jesus Christ and revealed to some by means of the Spirit's application of the gospel.

The gospel is revealed as God's eternal counsel

Fifth, the wisdom revealed in the gospel was "predestined before the ages to our glory" (v. 7b). The word "predestined" means "to decide beforehand."[17] God's gospel is understandable only through divine revelation because it originated in His eternal mind, which finite man cannot know unless God chooses to reveal Himself. Our sovereign God predestined the events of the crucifixion long before they ever occurred. Peter preached of this at Pentecost: "For truly in this city there were gathered together against Your holy servant Jesus, whom You anointed, both Herod and Pontius Pilate, along with the Gentiles and the peoples of Israel, *to do whatever Your hand and Your purpose predestined to occur*" (Acts 4:27–28). God predetermined in eternity past to use wicked rulers to fulfill His plan so that His Son would be crucified and the price of man's redemption paid. This plan was "to our glory," a reference to the completeness of our salvation in Christ.[18] Paul is confident of this when he writes to the believers in Rome, "For I consider that the sufferings of this present time are not worthy to be compared with the *glory* that is to be revealed to us" (Rom. 8:18). Leon Morris affirms, "Before time began God was concerned for our well-being; he planned the gospel that would bring us into glory."[19] In other words, God's redemptive plan is for His glory, but will surely lead to our glory, that is, our ultimate glorification in the presence of the Savior (1 John 3:2).

The gospel is not understandable to the unaided
Sixth and finally, "None of the rulers of this age has understood" God's wisdom (v. 8). "Understood" comes from the word meaning "to know, to recognize, to discern."[20] Paul then offers proof of this lack of understanding: "for if they had understood it, they would not have crucified the Lord of glory." In other words, if the rulers who crucified Jesus had possessed true wisdom, they would not have put Him to death. In Acts 3:17, after healing the lame beggar, Peter said to the Jews who were present, "I know that you acted in ignorance, just as your rulers did also." In John 16:3, predicting the persecution of His disciples, Jesus said, "These things they will do because they have not known the Father or Me." On the cross, Jesus prayed, "Father, forgive them; for they do not know what they are doing" (Luke 23:34).

The rulers of Jesus' day could not understand the plan of an infinite God. However, that did not excuse them. The religious leaders knew the Old Testament and still failed to see the man who stood before them as the Messiah they had longed for, so they crucified "the Lord of glory." Filled with self-righteousness and spiritual pride, they were blinded from seeing their King. In the same way, God keeps the life-transforming gospel hidden from the minds of those determined to justify themselves through their own efforts at self-improvement; "just as it is written, 'Things which eye has not seen and ear has not heard, and which have not entered the heart of man, all that God has prepared for those who love Him.'" Paul is again driving home his main point: God's revelation cannot be understood by human wisdom. How then can anyone know God? How can His wisdom enter the heart of man? It must be revealed to him by the Holy Spirit.

GOD'S WISDOM REVEALED BY THE HOLY SPIRIT (1 COR. 2:10–16)

For to us God revealed them through the Spirit; for the Spirit searches all things, even the depths of God. For who among men knows the thoughts of a man except the spirit of the man which is in him? Even so the thoughts of God no one knows except the Spirit of God. Now we have received, not the spirit of the world, but the Spirit who is from God, so that we may know the things freely given to us by God, which things we also speak, not in words taught by human wisdom, but in those taught by the Spirit, combining spiritual thoughts with spiritual words. But a natural man does not accept the things of the Spirit of God, for they are foolishness to him; and he cannot understand them, because they are spiritually appraised. But he who is spiritual appraises all things, yet he himself is appraised by no one. For who has known the mind of the Lord, that he should instruct Him? But we have the mind of Christ.

By nature, man cannot know "all that God has prepared for those who love Him" (v. 9). Therefore, he must have the wisdom of God revealed "through the Spirit" (v. 10). The phrase "to those who love Him" is another way of saying "to believers" (compare Rom. 8:28). Since God is the only one who knows what He has prepared for His people, He is the only One who can reveal it to them. Paul now shifts his thinking from *what* God has chosen to reveal to *how* He has chosen to disclose His wisdom. Specifically, the focus is on the ministry of the Holy Spirit. Here, Paul reveals three characteristics of the Spirit's ministry.

The Holy Spirit is the agent of revelation
First, the Holy Spirit is the member of the Trinity responsible for the revelation of truth. He is the one who reveals "them" (v. 10*a*), that is, the truths of God's wisdom, just as Jesus promised: "But when He, the Spirit of truth, comes, He will guide you into all the truth; for He will not speak on His own initiative, but whatever He hears, He will speak; and He will

disclose to you what is to come. He will glorify Me, for He will take of Mine and *will disclose it to you*" (John 16:13–14). The Holy Spirit does not invent truth along the way, but only reveals that which is consistent with Christ, the eternal and living Word. The truth of God concerning Jesus Christ cannot be known apart from God's sovereign choice to reveal Himself through His Word in the power of the Spirit. The truths of the gospel are hidden from the wise of this world, but to believers, "God revealed them through the Spirit."

The Holy Spirit knows the thoughts of God

Second, "the Spirit searches all things, even the depths of God" because He *is* God (v. 10). Only the Holy Spirit can plumb "the depth of the riches both of the wisdom and knowledge of God! How unsearchable are His judgments and unfathomable His ways!" (Rom. 11:33). It is humanly impossible to know the deep ways of God, but the Spirit knows them. In verse 11, Paul uses a human example to illustrate this spiritual truth: "who among men knows the thoughts of a man except the spirit of the man which is in him?" No man can know the thoughts of another man. He can only really know the thoughts of his own mind. However, he can know the mind of another man if that man chooses to reveal it to him. So it is with God: "Even so the thoughts of God no one knows except the Spirit of God." Just as the spirit of a man is the one who knows a man's mind, so the Spirit of God is One who knows the mind of God. Therefore, to know the mind of God requires that we possess the Spirit of God. He is our indispensable link to God's revelation.

The Holy Spirit has been given to believers

Third, the apostle reveals an amazing truth: believers have not received "the spirit of the world, but the Spirit who is from God" (v. 12). The word "world" comes from *kosmos*, which refers to the system of order governed by human wisdom and reason that is "in alienation from and opposition to God."[21] We do not need to even be tempted to place our confidence in the worldly teachings of men because we possess the Spirit of God Himself. He is God's gift to us so that we may know the truth. Paul explains four results of this gift.

Spirit-written revelation

The first result of the gift of the Spirit is that believers possess God's mind in written form. The apostle preached not "in words taught by human wisdom, but in those taught by the Spirit" (v. 13). By inspiration, the Holy Spirit gave forth the very words that were recorded as Scripture. When tempted, Jesus answered Satan, "It is written, 'Man shall not live on bread alone, but on *every word* that proceeds out of the mouth of God'" (Matt. 4:4). Paul was confident that he and the other apostles did not communicate the spiritual truths revealed to them by mere human authority, but rather in "demonstration of the Spirit and of power" (v. 4). "Combining spiritual thoughts with spiritual words" (v. 13) refers to explaining the things of the Spirit in the words of the Spirit, that is, using the Word of God to explain spiritual truths by using the Spirit's own words recorded for us in the Bible.

Spiritual judgment

The second result of the giving of the Spirit is that the withholding of illumination is a mark of God's judgment on unbelievers (v. 14). The unbeliever, the "natural" man, is "the worldly person."[22] This is the man who is wise in the things of this world, but totally inept in spiritual matters because he is bound by the limits of his own mind. The worldly-wise unbeliever does not "accept" the things of the Spirit. In the original Greek, this word can mean "to take up in one's arms."[23] In other words, unregenerate man does not naturally welcome biblical truth. According to Charles Hodge, not to accept the things of the Spirit is "not to receive them, is not to recognize, in our inward experience, their truth, authority, and excellence."[24] Instead of bowing to the authority of God's words, the unsaved consider them absurd because "they are spiritually appraised." The word "appraised" comes from a verb which means "to examine and judge, to call to account, to discern."[25] Those devoid of the Holy Spirit cannot discern spiritual truth because they do not possess the indwelling Divine Interpreter and Author of Scripture. They are like blind people trying to judge the paintings of Van Gogh. However, not only does the natural man not welcome spiritual truth, but also he cannot receive it with mere human intellect. Jesus said, "He who is of God hears the words of God; for this reason you do not hear them, because you are not of God" (John 8:47). Until the Spirit of God opens the spiritual eyes of unbelievers and brings understanding to the human heart, men and women cannot know God's saving power.

Spiritual discernment

The third result of the gift of the Spirit is the capacity to discern spiritual matters: "But he who is spiritual appraises all things" (v. 15). The "spiritual" man is the believer under the control of the Holy Spirit, as opposed to the natural man under the control of the fleshly mind, dominated by human wisdom. The Apostle John wrote of the believer's anointing of the Spirit: "As for you, the anointing which you received from Him abides in you, and you have no need for anyone to teach you; but as His anointing teaches you about all things, and is true and is not a lie, and just as it has taught you, you abide in Him" (1 John 2:27). As a result, the spiritual man "is appraised by no one" (1 Cor. 2:15). Paul and John were not teaching that some believers are above teaching or correction, or that they are not to be held accountable to the standard of Scripture. Instead, they were convinced that the believer cannot be properly judged by the natural man because the unbeliever does not have the Holy Spirit, the very One who gives the ability to discern, appreciate, and embrace the biblical truth that governs the believer's life.

Spiritual mind

The fourth and last result of the gift of the Spirit is that He enables believers to possess "the mind of Christ" (v. 16). Paul quotes from Isaiah 40:13 to further emphasize the human impossibility of knowing the mind of God. He asks, "For who has known the mind of the Lord, that he will instruct Him?", then boldly declares, "But we have the mind of Christ." Though the natural man cannot comprehend the truth of God, the Christian can, because he or she has been given the Spirit of Jehovah. This same Holy Spirit is the believer's chief Counselor. Jesus promised, "But the Helper, the Holy Spirit, whom the Father will send in My name, He will teach you all things, and bring to your remembrance all that I said to you" (John 14:26). The Holy Spirit is the One sent alongside believers to teach us spiritual truth using the words that He inspired. The Bible is the mind of God in written form. It is the mind of Christ!

Since Scripture is the mind of Christ, it is the final standard of truth and the absolute authority for faith and practice. The integration of psychology and theology is nothing less than an admission of a lack of confidence in the sufficiency of the Word of God. For that reason, biblical counselors must be faithful to engage in active combat with every form of human wisdom "raised up against the knowledge of God" (2 Cor. 10:5).

God's wisdom victorious

> For though we walk in the flesh, we do not war according to the flesh, for the weapons of our warfare are not of the flesh, but divinely powerful for the destruction of fortresses. We are destroying speculations and every lofty thing raised up against the knowledge of God, and we are taking every thought captive to the obedience of Christ, and we are ready to punish all disobedience, whenever your obedience is complete.
>
> 2 Cor. 10:3–6

Regardless of the subtlety of Christian psychology's assault, or of the sincerity of its advocates, it is an attack on the sufficiency of Christ nonetheless. In this passage, we sense the apostle's passion for biblical truth as he describes the mode (vv. 3–4) and means (vv. 5–6) of the warfare in which biblical counselors find themselves engaged.

THE MODE OF WARFARE

Paul makes it clear that the "warfare" in which believers in Christ are involved is a well-thought-out "campaign."[26] The word he uses is *strateia*, from which we get "strategy." Specifically, the devil's battle against Christ-centered wisdom is not an accident. Satan specializes in disguising himself as "an angel of light" (2 Cor. 11:14). Therefore, the invasion of psychology into the church is a well-planned and well-executed war against the sufficiency of Christ and His Word.

The weapons of this war are "not of the flesh." In other words, the war is spiritual, not physical or earthly (Eph. 6:10–17). It is not against men, but against the *wisdom* of men; "though we walk in the flesh, we do not war according to the flesh." Our weapons in this realm are "divinely powerful"; that is, they are empowered by God for the purpose of pulling down "fortresses." These fortresses are strongholds of the mind, built by the bricks of false philosophy which are "raised up against" Christ. As mental prisons, they hold people captive.

Consequently, the war exists in the realm of ideas that become doctrines, which may then be taught to men as if they were the truth. Colossians

2:8 warns, "See to it that no one takes you captive through philosophy and empty deception, according to the tradition of men, according to the elementary principles of the world, rather than according to Christ." How are the disobedient held captive? Through false doctrines, as the wisdom of man devalues Jesus Christ and diminishes the power of His gospel. Christian psychology has succeeded in spreading false principles in which far too many believers have now placed their trust. Biblical counselors must carefully identify and attack these mental prisons and, like the wise man who "scales the city of the mighty," we must "[bring] down the stronghold in which they trust" (Prov. 21:22).

THE MEANS OF WARFARE

Since the battle is not physical but philosophical and spiritual, the weapons used to pull down these mental prisons that enslave people must also be in the form of spiritual teachings, doctrines, worldviews, and principles. By consistently teaching the sufficiency of Jesus Christ and the application of His Word to every area of life, we destroy "speculations," or "reasonings" or "thoughts."[27] We must actively oppose ideologies that glorify man rather than Christ. We must combat "every lofty thing," every arrogant "obstacle"[28] which Satan, the deceiver, uses to keep people from devotion to Jesus. We must take every thought captive to the obedience of Christ. There is only one sure way to do that. We must judge every teaching by the standard of the written Word of Christ. We must "test the spirits to see whether they are from God" (1 John 4:1). As we do so, those we disciple will grow to maturity and "have their senses trained to discern good and evil" (Heb. 5:14). We must also be ready to call all teachers to account for the error of their "disobedience." David Wells' assessment of the current state of the church is correct: "many in the Church have now turned in upon themselves and substituted for the knowledge of God a search for the knowledge of self."[29] Nothing has contributed more to the current preoccupation with self than the propagation of a psychological gospel.

Perhaps no man has popularized this man-centered approach to Christianity more than radio psychologist James Dobson. Setting aside any question of his sincerity or personal integrity, it must be recognized, however, that his media ministry has been more responsible for spreading the Christ-diminishing gospel of self-esteem, self-love, self-respect, and self-acceptance than many others. For over three decades, *Focus on the Family* has been beating the self-esteem drum with a passion. Unfortunately, as much as Dr. Dobson's enduring fight for morality and the preservation of traditional family values is deeply appreciated by all who love and serve Christ, his fundamental view of man's need is erroneous and, therefore, subtly undermines biblical foundations. In his book *Hide or Seek: How to Build Self-Esteem in Your Child*, he clearly states that a low view of self, not the total depravity of man, is the fundamental cause of the problems in our society. Dobson writes,

> In a real sense, the health of an entire society depends on the ease with which its individual members can gain personal acceptance. *Thus, whenever the keys to self-esteem are seemingly out of reach for a large percentage of the people, as in twentieth-century America, then widespread "mental illness," neuroticism, hatred, alcoholism, drug abuse, violence, and social disorder will certainly occur.*[30]

Later in the same book, he adds, "social chaos of all varieties is rooted in feelings of worthlessness during the early years of childhood."[31] Finally, he is convinced that "Many of the seemingly unsolvable social problems we are now facing represent desperate but unsuccessful attempts to cope with inferiority. When the incidence of self-doubt is greatest, accompanied by the unavailability of acceptable solutions, then the probability of irresistible social disorder is maximized. Call it Dobson's Law, if you wish."[32]

The question every believer must ask is: How does "Dobson's Law" measure up against the law of God in Scripture? Is a lack of self-esteem the root cause of social chaos? The Apostle Paul responds, "Hardly!" Instead, the Word of God incorporates self-love into its list of the evil ways in which the total depravity of man will display itself in the end times. Second Timothy 3:1–5 says,

> But realize this, that in the last days difficult times will come. For men will be lovers of self, lovers of money, boastful, arrogant, revilers, disobedient to parents, ungrateful, unholy, unloving, irreconcilable, malicious gossips, without self-control, brutal, haters of good, treacherous, reckless, conceited, lovers of pleasure rather than lovers of God, holding to a form of godliness, although they have denied its power; avoid such men as these.

When comparing "Dobson's Law" (man's root problem is a low view of self) with God's law (man's root problem is his idolatrous self), it is obvious they are solar systems apart. Rather than identifying self-doubt, or low self-esteem, as the source of society's ills, the apostle says the problem is that men are "lovers of self." And depraved man is not filled with self-doubt, he is "boastful" and "arrogant." Self-love is nothing short of idolatry, the worship of self, the core problem that Jesus came to deliver us from.

Someone may well say, "Surely you do not believe Dr. Dobson is solely responsible for the spread of integrationism!" No, I do not. There are dozens of other prominent speakers and writers preaching different angles of the same self-fulfillment gospel. However, it must be acknowledged that the popularity of his media ministry has without a doubt provided a worldwide platform for the spread of Christian psychology. As a result, Dobson serves as an effective illustration of the modern shift away from a biblical emphasis on the person and redemptive work of Jesus Christ toward a message that addresses man's alleged psychological needs which, in the end, glorify self—not Christ. In short, the gospel of integrationism has changed Jesus our Savior into Jesus our therapist.

Summary
The integration of psychology and Christian theology is flawed on at least two basic levels. First, integrationists have one common problem—too high a view of man. And in having too high a view of man, the integrationist fails to recognize that man's deepest problem is not unmet psychological needs, but the waywardness of a heart that is totally depraved and at enmity with God. The damage this false gospel has caused within professing Christianity is incalculable. If man's greatest need is personal acceptance rather than personal redemption from the personal guilt of personal sinfulness, then the message of the cross of Jesus Christ is made void. Therefore, battle against worldly psychology is imperative.

Second, Christian psychology is flawed because it reveals a loyalty to man's wisdom as opposed to a pure, childlike trust in the Word of God. In reality, it is nothing short of a subtle strategy of Satan to keep the gospel of Christ hidden from men by cloaking it within the arrogance of human wisdom. When human wisdom is blended with the pure truth of Christ, the result is only confusion and the supplanting of faith in the sufficiency of Scripture with trust in man. Therefore, Powlison's assessment of integrationists is correct:

Integrationists attempt to wed secular psychology to conservative Christianity because they believe that Scripture is not comprehensively sufficient. Scripture, the Word of the Holy Spirit, is in some essential way deficient for understanding and changing people. The church, therefore, needs systematic and constitutive input from the social sciences in order to know what is true and to enable effective, loving counseling ministry. Integrationists aim to import the intellectual contents and psychotherapeutic practices of psychology into the church in a way that is consistent with biblical faith.[33]

However, as we have seen in this chapter, this marriage of truth and error cannot be carried out without compromising the gospel, since the foundations of theology and psychology are so drastically different. In fact, they are from different worlds.

Christian psychology offers nothing needful to the practice of biblical counseling because its fundamental views of man, his deepest needs, and the means by which he can and must change, are erroneous. Therefore, the integration of psychology with theology must continue to be opposed by all those who truly hold to the sufficiency of Jesus Christ and His inerrant Word. Biblical counselors have a choice to make. Either the revelation of God in His Word is fully trustworthy and complete, or it is inadequate and, therefore, in need of help from human wisdom. The curse and the promise of God through Jeremiah the prophet serve as a fitting conclusion:

> Thus says the LORD,
> "Cursed is the man who trusts in mankind
> And makes flesh his strength,
> And whose heart turns away from the LORD.
> For he will be like a bush in the desert
> And will not see when prosperity comes,
> But will live in stony wastes in the wilderness,
> A land of salt without inhabitant.
> Blessed is the man who trusts in the LORD
> And whose trust is the LORD.
> For he will be like a tree planted by the water,
> That extends its roots by a stream
> And will not fear when the heat comes;
> But its leaves will be green,

> And it will not be anxious in a year of drought
> Nor cease to yield fruit."

Jer. 17:5–8

Trusting God means trusting His revelation in the written Word, the Bible. To turn away from His truth in order to embrace man's theories, or to attempt to mix the two, is to place one's trust in mankind. As a result, the blessing of fruitfulness from the Lord is lost and, in its place, spiritual barrenness is experienced. But this is not God's will for His church. Instead, God has designed His church to be a community where stimulating, Christ-centered faith is continually nurtured.

For further thought and small-group discussion

1. Read 2 Corinthians 11:2–3. Discuss the Apostle Paul's burden. Why was he so grieved?

2. Read James 3:13–18. Discuss the difference between man's wisdom and the wisdom of God. How do their outworkings differ?

3. Read 1 Corinthians 2:10–16. Discuss the essential ministry of the Holy Spirit to help us understand Scripture. What is the "mind of Christ," and why does Paul say that believers possess it?

4. Read 1 Corinthians 1:18. Discuss the meaning of the phrase "the word of the cross." Why does Paul teach that the cross is the center of God's revelation?

5. Read Philippians 2:3–8. What should replace our inborn self-esteem? How did Jesus model humility and "others-esteem"? Why is self-love not a virtue?

The community for stimulating faith

stimulating faith

Chapter 8

Therefore, brethren, since we have confidence to enter the holy place by the blood of Jesus, by a new and living way which He inaugurated for us through the veil, that is, His flesh, and since we have a great priest over the house of God, let us draw near with a sincere heart in full assurance of faith, having our hearts sprinkled clean from an evil conscience and our bodies washed with pure water. Let us hold fast the confession of our hope without wavering, for He who promised is faithful; and let us consider how to stimulate one another to love and good deeds, not forsaking our own assembling together, as is the habit of some, but encouraging one another; and all the more as you see the day drawing near.

–Heb. 10:19–25

Authentic biblical counseling requires the nurturing power of stimulating relationships with other Spirit-indwelt believers in the context of a community of living faith that pursues the beauty of God's holiness and revolves around the redeeming sacrifice of Jesus Christ. God's vision of discipleship, then, requires that it be cross-driven and church-based, because growth, sanctification, and progress in godliness necessitate Christ-centered relationships. This kind of fellowship transcends all superficial distinctions, such as age or marital status, and instead promotes spiritual growth through cross-generational, same-gender mentoring. Consequently, we must be committed to the priority of the local church in the life of every disciple and tirelessly work to return counseling to its rightful place.

Regrettably, some professing believers either do not recognize their need of others or no longer see the importance of faithfulness to one assembly of believers, and have chosen instead to pursue something more to their individual liking. In his book *Stop Dating the Church*, Joshua Harris demonstrates the boldness to write what many of us have been too timid to even whisper in private admonishment to fellow believers: that Christians who are uncommitted to a fellowship of believers are disobedient to God, and that believers whose operative attitude is "serve me" know nothing of the self-denial of the cross-driven life.

Yet that is right where much of our "Christian" subculture lives. There are far too many professing believers living disconnected from, or uncommitted to, the local church. "Cafeteria Christians" is what they've been called for decades. This is the age of the buffet—get as much as you can for the cheapest price; in other words, the most amenities for the least commitment. Unfortunately, many Christians don't see the fallacy of this line of thinking. Never would the believers in the New Testament have entertained such a strange notion! The normal Christianity of the early church was tenacious in its commitment to biblical fellowship. What constituted healthy discipleship was a strong commitment to sound teaching, the accountability of biblical fellowship, the priority of the cross, and utter dependence on God in prayer within the context of community (Acts 2:42).

But that is not what the typical church-hopper is looking for today. So, like the recreational dater who has already "dumped" half a dozen potential mates, many of today's Christians simply change churches when the grass begins to look greener elsewhere. Sometimes, it's a clean, decisive break in relationship because they are simply tired of being called to the self-death that Jesus requires of His disciples. Other times, they begin flirting around and are gradually drawn away by fancier programs, more entertaining music, or less convicting, therapeutic, ego-stroking preaching. Whichever surface motivations are involved, what should be of great concern are the immature, fleshly priorities that seem to drive too many of today's Christians.

In Harris's helpful little book, he provides what he calls "the profile of a church dater," in other words, the person who wants all the benefits and image of church association without the discipline of real commitment. He challenges all of us to examine ourselves to see if we have inadvertently picked up any aspects of this mentality. If we are church daters, Harris says, we possess at least one of three attitudes:

- First, our attitudes toward church tend to be *me-centered*. We go for what we can get—social interaction, programs, or activities. The driving question is, "What can church do for me?"
- A second sign of a church dater is being *independent*. We go to

church because that's what Christians are supposed to do—but we're careful to avoid getting involved too much, especially with people. We don't pay much attention to God's larger purpose for us as a vital part in a specific church family. So we go through the motions without really investing ourselves.

- Most essentially, a church dater tends to be *critical*. We are short on allegiance and quick to find fault in our churches. We treat church with a consumer mentality—looking for the best product for the price of our Sunday morning. As a result, we're fickle and not invested for the long term, like a lover with a wandering eye, always on the hunt for something better.[1]

It is clear that this is not what the apostles envisioned the believer's relationship to the local church to be. Consequently, it is time for Christians to regain a biblical understanding of the important role that an assembly of believers should have in their lives. The sooner we learn that we are not called to be consumers on the hunt for the best buy, but worshippers in pursuit of a closer walk of obedience to our holy God, the better off we will be.

Perhaps one of the more subtle ways Christians forsake the church is by succumbing to, or promoting, the professionalization of counseling. These believers don't necessarily leave their churches physically, but they do so emotionally through divided loyalty. Worse yet, they often adopt the mindset that no one in their churches, including their pastors, can possibly understand the deep struggles of their souls and their quests for "inner healing." As a result, they often keep their distance from the very people within the church to whom they are biblically accountable, and instead become transparently honest with the professional counselors outside the church whose answers are rarely questioned due to the psychological degrees hanging on their office walls. This simply is not God's plan for discipleship, as David Powlison says so well:

> Soul care and soul cure—sustaining sufferers and transforming sinners—is a vital part of the ministry of the church according to the Bible, however poorly we may be doing the job … Extramural Christian works need to remember that they are "barely legitimate" in the sense that they ought to exist only when they genuinely and intentionally serve the interests of the communities whose mature functioning will put them out of business. For example, para-church

ministry becomes illegitimate when it competes with or uses local churches to its own ends ... I believe that to organize counseling according to the mental health professional model is fundamentally, even disastrously, wrong. At the same time, truly wise church-oriented counseling ministry is decades away for the church as a whole ... We must each labor to dismantle autonomous professionalism rather than reinforce it. We must each labor to make our loyalty to the church a significant reality rather than a mere statement of good intentions.[2]

In other words, every para-church business or ministry that may provide assistance in the discipleship process (e.g. Bible colleges, seminaries, counseling training centers, publishing houses, etc.) finds legitimacy for its existence only in its connection to, and support of, the ministry of reproductive churches.[3]

In spite of all its flaws and less-than-perfect members and pastors, churches remain God's ordained communities of the faith and centers for biblical counseling. I am intentionally using the descriptive phrase "community of the faith," along with "local church" in this chapter to emphasize the priority of Christ-centered relationships grounded in biblical doctrine. Other New Testament pictures of the church include that of "the bride of Christ" (Eph. 5:25; Rev. 21:2), which highlights the believer's relationship with Jesus; and "a called-out assembly" (James 2:2), which accentuates the believer's relationship to the world; but "community" is an essential picture as well, since it stresses the need for believers to live together spiritually, united by truth, and in a close association of mutual care, rather than independently, as "spiritual Lone Rangers."[4] These spiritual communities are God's ordained instruments for carrying out the Great Command, and will continue to be so until Jesus returns. Therefore, we must lead followers of Christ toward a stronger commitment to their local assemblies where they can grow in the grace and knowledge of their Savior Jesus Christ and practice biblical love by learning to serve others. In a nutshell, God's instruction in Hebrews 10:19–25 must be studied and obeyed.

The basis for community

Life-transforming fellowship with other believers is based upon three significant truths. The first concerns the exalted position of Jesus Christ, while the other two truths are cross-driven privileges that every believer possesses. Here we see the centrality of the gospel in biblical fellowship, or community.

THE PREEMINENCE OF JESUS CHRIST

The book of Hebrews is unique in that it is one of the inspired books whose author is unknown. The exact reason for his anonymity is not revealed, but Edmond Hiebert offers a worthy explanation:

> The more we contemplate this enigma concerning the authorship of this marvelous revelation of the supremacy of our Lord Jesus Christ, the more we feel that our ignorance is divinely intended to direct our attention rather to the message of the book. In this Spirit-breathed book the attention is centered upon Christ. He must ever remain preeminent. Throughout the epistle the unnamed author refrains from any mention of men, except to set them aside if they come at all, in the minds of the readers, in competition with Christ.[5]

This Christ-exalting book was written between AD 65–68, before the destruction of the temple in Jerusalem (otherwise the author undoubtedly would have mentioned the ruins as proof of the completion of the Old Testament sacrificial system). The author's immediate audience was made up of faltering Jewish Christians within a specific congregation of people, evidenced by the desire of the author to visit them soon (13:19, 23).

The book's purpose is to encourage, warn, and instruct readers experiencing spiritual erosion. The author warns his readers of the dangers of apostasy and encourages them to maintain their boldness and confidence in the faith. Some had wanted to return to the Law because they did not recognize the fullness of their standing in Christ and thus were failing to experience their new life as God intended.

The theme of the book is the superiority of Christ our High Priest, as seen in the use of such key words as "better," "perfect," "heavenly," and "forever" to exalt Jesus above the old system of animal sacrifice. Many unbelievers were wavering between receiving and rejecting Jesus as Messiah, and those who were believers needed to be convinced of His sufficiency and learn to rest in Him. Hiebert notes,

> The persecutions they had formerly endured had died down. But with the favorable change in the circumstances had come a dangerous change in them. They were experiencing spiritual degeneration, having "become dull

of hearing" (Heb 5:11), they needed again to be cared for as spiritual babies (5:12–14). There was danger of them drifting away from the things they had heard (2:1). They needed to be warned against "an evil heart of unbelief, in falling away from the living God" (3:12). They had become worldly minded (13:5) and there was a tendency among them to forsake their assembling together (10:25).[6]

Hebrews 10 serves as a transition from doctrine to exhortation. Here we find the basis for, and building blocks of, a community of faith-filled believers that becomes an atmosphere providing stimulation for the progress of discipleship.

THE PRIVILEGE OF ENTRY INTO GOD'S PRESENCE

The first great privilege is set apart by the words "Therefore ... since" (v. 19). In other words, the author is exhorting his readers, "Since you are New-Covenant people and the Old Testament sacrifices were brought to completion at the cross of Calvary, you should be coming into the presence of God with confidence." "Confidence" also means "boldness [or] assurance."[7] It is translated "openness" in Acts 28:31 with reference to the courage of Paul's preaching, and "confidence" in 1 John 2:28, referring to not shrinking away from Christ at His Second Coming. In other words, believers have the privilege of entering God's presence with assurance because the basis of our entrance is not what we have done, but "the blood of Jesus."

Through Him we enter "the holy place," a structure set apart to God. According to *A Linguistic Key to the Greek New Testament*, "The expression designates the innermost sanctuary of the Holy of Holies into which, under the old dispensation, the people were forbidden to enter."[8] Though in the Old Testament only the high priest could enter this place once a year, this New Testament book reveals its fulfillment in Jesus Christ, thus opening continual access to God to every sinner who comes by faith.

> For Christ did not enter a holy place made with hands, a mere copy of the true one, but into heaven itself, now to appear in the presence of God for us; nor was it that He would offer Himself often, as the high priest enters the holy place year by year with blood that is not his own. Otherwise, He would have needed to suffer often since the foundation of the world; but now once at the

consummation of the ages He has been manifested to put away sin by the sacrifice of Himself.

9:24–26

As High Priest, Jesus entered the holy place to offer a one-time sacrifice for His people. He offered Himself as the perfect payment for man's sin and thus God's holy standard was satisfied and His wrath propitiated (Rom. 3:25). Now, all who approach God by faith in Christ may enter with assurance because we enter through His merit alone.

According to Hebrews 10:1–14, the old system was inadequate because it could "never, by the same sacrifices … year by year, make perfect those who draw near" (v. 1). There was no way for man to fully remedy his sin problem by means of animal sacrifice. If the offerings had really done the job, they would have "ceased to be offered" (v. 2). But they were not complete. Instead, they pointed to the one true altar on the hill called Calvary. God's promise of a Redeemer that demonstrates His righteousness by making full atonement for sin is the reason why He "passed over the sins previously committed" (Rom. 3:25). Therefore, the Son of God said to the Father, "Sacrifice and offering You have not desired, but a body You have prepared for Me" (Heb. 10:5). He alone is the fulfillment of every one of the millions of animals that were slain for the progress of redemption.

In Christ, believers have the privilege of entering into the presence of God by a "new and living way" (10:20). "Thus the sacrifice of Jesus is forever regarded as having just been made. It shall never lose its power."9 "The word indicates 'fresh,' not only in the sense that it is a way which was before unknown, but also as one that retains its freshness and cannot grow old."10 Therefore, Jesus remains the newly slain one who is able to free us from sin's penalty and power by giving us His spiritual freedom and life.

This new way came through "the veil, that is, His flesh." As the veil in the tabernacle of Israel barred man's access into the Holy of Holies as long as it remained intact, so the humanity of Christ prevented the sinner's access to God until it was torn at the cross. Jesus had to suffer a physical death as well as endure spiritual separation from the Father (Matt. 27:46). He had to be a perfect sacrifice to appease the wrath of God and satisfy His justice. During the crucifixion, "the veil of the temple was torn in two from top to bottom" (Matt 27:51). By removing this barrier, God declared to the world that sinners can now come to Him anytime through His Son. In Him, we possess the right to immediate and bold entrance into the holiest of places—the very presence of God.

A community of faith that is a favorable environment for biblical counseling will never lose its sense of wonder over the greatness of the sacrifice of Jesus, which freely purchased immediate and continual access into the presence of God for repentant sinners. This is surely one of the reasons why Jesus instructs us to frequently remember His sacrifice by means of the visual object lesson called the Lord's Table (Luke 22:19–20; 1 Cor. 11:24–25). While participating, we identify ourselves with the slain body and spilled blood of our Savior. Our sin has been atoned for by Jesus Christ. "Therefore, having been justified by faith, we have peace with God through our Lord Jesus Christ, through whom also we have obtained our introduction by faith into this grace in which we stand; and we exult in hope of the glory of God" (Rom. 5:1–2). This is the first privilege that forms the basis of corporate fellowship in the community of faith.

THE POSSESSION OF A GREAT HIGH PRIEST

The second great privilege that forms the basis of community among believers is the possession of a "great priest over the house of God" (Heb. 10:21). Christ is the eternal, living intercessor for God's household, the church. As believers, our confidence is based upon the fact that we have a High Priest who always lives to make intercession for us (Heb. 7:25). Hebrews 4:14–16 says,

> Therefore, since we have a great high priest who has passed through the heavens, Jesus the Son of God, let us hold fast our confession. For we do not have a high priest who cannot sympathize with our weaknesses, but One who has been tempted in all things as we are, yet without sin. Therefore let us draw near with confidence to the throne of grace, so that we may receive mercy and find grace to help in time of need.

Believers possess a Mediator who has already satisfied the holy wrath of God against our sin. As a result, we can boldly come to the Father in Jesus' name. But Jesus is also a sympathetic priest because there is no temptation that we face that He did not resist. Knowing this should cause us to draw near to Him in time of need. His throne is a "throne of grace," dispensing mercy and help to us whenever we call for it in the face of testing.

However, if we would listen to our own prayers this kind of confidence is seldom heard. Instead, our timid approach often communicates the fear that perhaps God won't listen to us. We must learn to pray with humble faith and courage, realizing who we are in Christ. Jesus is not ashamed to call us His brethren (Heb. 2:11). As a result, we can now approach the throne of God saying, "I come with boldness not because of myself, but because of Christ. Therefore, hear my prayer."

In summary, a community of faith that is conducive to biblical counseling will relentlessly teach disciples how to pray and how to make the practice of prayer a priority in their Christian lives. We must remind ourselves of the surety of our standing in Christ our High Priest, whose mediatorial work did not end at the cross. Instead, He lives today and "His divine power has granted to us everything pertaining to life and godliness, through the true knowledge of Him who called us by His own glory and excellence" (2 Peter 1:3). There is no reason to look outside the provision He has already made. The basis for Christian fellowship is the privileged access we have to God in Christ. This is what unifies disciples.

Having established this, the writer now moves on to reveal the building blocks that make up a spiritual community that stimulates us toward maturity in Christ.

The building blocks of community

There are three essential building blocks in a community of the biblical faith. When we gather together as an assembly of Christ-followers, these building blocks must be present in order for God to be pleased with our worship and fellowship.

DRAWING NEAR IN WORSHIP

For God to be pleased, disciples must "draw near" to Him in worship (Heb. 10:22), which necessitates the meeting of four conditions. Believers must meet the first two demands, but Christ has already satisfied the latter two. Let's look first at the requirements that we must meet.

A *true heart*

We must first draw near "with a sincere heart." The word "sincere" means true or dependable.[11] It is more than simple sincerity, though it includes this. Many religious people come to God in sincerity, but not in truth. Our God demands both. A true heart is every believer's responsibility when gathering together with other believers as a church family. Therefore, before we worship, we ought to make sure that we are each coming to our assembly with a genuine heart that has confronted our own hypocrisy and known sin. If conflict exists between us and another believer, we must take the initiative to make it right, even on the way to the corporate worship service if necessary (Matt. 5:23–24; Rom. 12:18).

A true heart is also undivided. The psalmist asked, "Who may ascend into the hill of the LORD? And who may stand in His holy place? He who has clean hands and a pure heart" (Ps. 24:3–4). First Chronicles 12:33 mentions 50,000 soldiers who drew up in battle array and helped David "with an undivided heart." A true heart is not divided between God and the world, but is wholly dedicated to Him alone. In repentance, David prayed, "Behold, You desire truth in the innermost being" (Ps. 51:6). True worship begins with truth in the inner man.

A confident faith
The second condition to acceptable worship is coming to God "in full assurance of faith" (Heb. 10:22). The first readers of the book of Hebrews were lacking assurance because of their waning faith. Consequently, growth was needed to increase the confidence in and the assurance of their fellowship with God. In a later chapter we read, "without faith it is impossible to please Him, for he who comes to God must believe that He is and that He is a rewarder of those who seek Him" (11:6). To worship in faith is to come with a seeking heart that rests in the merit of Christ alone.

Drawing near to God in worship contains conditions that every believer is responsible for meeting. Disciple-makers must guard their own hearts as they prepare for public worship, but they must also help those they are counseling to deal honestly with sin and grow to confident faith in Christ as they continue to help them learn to think biblically and to apply the gospel to life. There are two more conditions, but the word "having" (Heb. 10:22) indicates that they have already been met by the atoning work of Jesus Christ.

A clean conscience
We can only come to God in sincerity of faith if our hearts have been

"sprinkled clean" (10:22). The word "sprinkle," in the passive voice, speaks of the purging of "the hearts of believers from an evil conscience."[12] It is in the perfect tense, which indicates a completed state or condition; in other words, guilt is gone. In Christ, the believer's conscience has already been cleansed of guilt. When a sinner comes to Jesus and receives salvation, guilt is removed.

Even if feelings of guilt remain, the actual legal guilt is gone because, in the body of His Son, God judged the sin that caused the guilt. "Therefore there is now no condemnation for those who are in Christ Jesus" (Rom. 8:1). Sometimes we as believers still experience guilty feelings over our past because we do not fully realize the extent of our cleansing. Therefore, we must continually speak the gospel to ourselves and to those we are counseling, so that we will learn to live in the freedom that already belongs to us in Christ. "He has not dealt with us according to our sins, nor rewarded us according to our iniquities" (Ps. 103:10).

A clean body

The word "washed" (10:22) is also in the perfect tense, indicating that it too is a requirement that has already been met. This condition, as well as the previous one, speaks of the Levitical ceremonies that prepared priests for service and both are symbolic of the process whereby they were sprinkled with the sacrificial blood and thoroughly washed before ministering to others. Whereas the priests had to repeat their cleansing annually on the Day of Atonement, believers now have permanent and direct access to God through Christ because we have been thoroughly cleansed by Him. John Calvin comments on this text:

> The meaning is, that we are made partakers of Christ, if we come to him, sanctified in body and soul; and yet that this sanctification is not what consists in a visible parade of ceremonies, but that it is from faith, pure conscience, and that cleanness of soul and body which flows from, and is effected by, the Spirit of God. So Paul exhorts the faithful to cleanse themselves from all filthiness of flesh and spirit, since they had been adopted by God as his children.[13]

Jesus said to Peter, "He who has bathed needs only to wash his feet, but is completely clean" (John 13:10). The atoning work of Christ is so complete that it continues to cleanse us. "If we say that we have fellowship with Him and yet walk in the darkness, we lie and do not practice the truth; but if we walk in the light as He Himself is in the light, we have fellowship with one another, and the blood of Jesus His Son cleanses us from all sin" (1 John 1:6–7). There is power in the blood of the Lamb of God. There is no sin that God will not wash away when we come to Him on His terms. To come to Him by faith means to relinquish all trust in self, realizing that there is no other hope for forgiveness. This is what God requires. "Now to the one who works, his wage is not credited as a favor, but as what is due. But to the one who does not work, but believes in Him who justifies the ungodly, his faith is credited as righteousness" (Rom. 4:4–5). When this empty-handed faith exists, complete cleansing becomes reality.

Therefore, as counselors, we must help disciples understand the fullness of their forgiveness in Christ. Without it, they cannot truly approach God in truth, sincerity, and confidence, and fully participate in the corporate worship of the church.

HOLDING FAST IN HOPE

In addition to drawing near to God in worship, the second building block of community is firmly holding fast to our common hope (10:23). The verb translated "hold fast" means "to hold fast, to possess."[14] Believers are to have a firm grip on "the confession of our hope." "Confession" (*homologia*) is an agreement. In other words, when we come together for corporate worship and fellowship, we agree on the source of our hope—Jesus Christ. We are to do this "without wavering" because "He who promised is faithful." Because of persecution, these Jewish believers were beginning to revert back to the old system. Consequently, the writer urged them to focus on the superiority of Christ instead.

We too have the tendency to lean back on human works and become performance-based in our faith. Rather, we must fix our eyes on Jesus, "the author and perfecter of faith" (Heb. 12:2). We must also continually reinforce the basis of our unity as Jesus Christ and avoid superficial distinctions that divide our community of faith. As helpful as it might be to occasionally segment off "singles" or "young marrieds" or "senior saints" for times of strategic teaching and relationship-building, a community of the faith must strive to be just that: a community of "the faith." My point is not to say that no such divisions may exist in the practical outworking of church life, but to emphasize the fact that all superficial distinctions should fade away as we continually exalt the Lord Jesus as the One who unites us and removes all earthly barriers to corporate fellowship.

ENCOURAGING GROWTH IN GODLINESS

The third building block of community is the mutual encouragement of believers toward Christlikeness that helps to prevent our own apostasy. This is essential since the capacity to leave the truth lies within every human heart. By nature, we are all like Demas, capable of falling in love with the temporal things of this world and deserting the work of Christ (2 Tim. 4:10). However, as we continually apply these Christ-centered truths and keep the implications of the cross evident in our relationships within the body, we feed one another's growth and perform preventive maintenance on our souls.

The writer of Hebrews continues, "let us consider" (10:24). The word "consider" means, "to place the mind down upon ... to consider thoughtfully."[15] In short, the writer is insisting that believers take careful note of one another's spiritual welfare. We are to keep an eye on one another, to hold one another accountable for our spiritual walks, because our common hope in Christ results in a binding relationship for mutual growth.

The purpose of this practice of biblical fellowship is "to stimulate one another." "Stimulate" comes from a word meaning "irritating, inciting, stimulation."[16] It is translated "disagreement" in Acts 15:39 with reference to the dispute between Paul and Barnabas. Solomon said, "Iron sharpens iron, so one man sharpens another" (Prov. 27:17). Believers are to *irritate* each other toward growth. This refers to a healthy tension that promotes growth, since biblical change normally takes place alongside other people. However, too many believers avoid difficult situations or people that challenge their thinking when, in reality, God intends to use others to move us toward spiritual maturity. Timothy Lane and Paul Tripp, in *How People Change*, observe,

> At one level we want friendships. At another level we don't want them! In creation, we were made to live in community, but because of the fall, we tend to run from the very friendships we need. Quite often, our longing for them is tainted by sin. We pursue them only as long as they satisfy our own desires and needs. We have a love–hate relationship with relationships! The

Bible recognizes this profound tension, but still places our individual growth in grace in the context of the body of Christ. The Scriptures call us to be intimately connected to our brothers and sisters in Christ. Our fellowship is an essential ingredient for lasting change. The work of redemption involves our individual relationship with Christ alongside our relationship with others … Many helpers fail to move struggling people into the rich context of redemptive relationships. Instead, they cling to the arid individualism of our society. They have a "Jesus and me" mindset as they battle sin and seek to become more like Christ.[17]

In contrast to the pride of individualism, God wants His people to be faithful in meeting together for the purpose of inciting one another "to love and good deeds." It is through this stimulus that believers help one another fulfill Ephesians 2:10: "we are His workmanship, created in Christ Jesus for good works, which God prepared beforehand so that we would walk in them."

The times when we are tempted to avoid others are the very times we need to be the most steadfastly committed to fellowship in the church. Mark Dever and Paul Alexander remind us, "We can't live the Christian life alone. We are saved individually from our sins, yet we are not saved into a vacuum. We're saved into a mutually edifying community of believers who are building each other up and spurring each other on to love and good deeds."[18] The church is a body consisting of many parts, none of which can thrive on its own (1 Cor. 12).

Nevertheless, there is a negative side to this building block. Believers are not to forsake regular fellowship (Heb. 10:25). "Forsaking" is a present active participle from a verb meaning "to leave behind."[19] The "assembling" that believers are not to be careless about refers to "the regular gathering together of Christian believers for worship and exhortation in a particular place."[20] Obviously, some were relaxing their involvement at the public meetings of the local church to the point where it was becoming a habit. Maybe they were once faithful and had gradually departed, but now they were experiencing spiritual decline because of lack of exposure to the Word of God and the stimulation of other believers. Proverbs 27:8 says, "like a bird that wanders from her nest, so is a man who wanders from his home." Some were short-circuiting their own sanctification because of a lax view of the priority of biblical fellowship.

For this reason, we must unequivocally teach that, to be obedient to God, every believer in Christ should be a member of a Bible-teaching local church. Every disciple needs spiritual leaders to equip him or her for ministry, and every disciple needs others in the family of God to serve and to be accountable to. We all have sharp edges that need to be smoothed by continual contact with others. To a great extent, our spiritual growth directly hinges upon it. Unfortunately, there is a growing movement of people who are completely abandoning the concept of a local assembly. These independent Christians are trying to live the Christian life in isolation like monks. In many cases, this neglect is the fruit of pride and self-will on the part of those who cannot bring themselves to serve others. Because they refuse to submit to one another or any spiritual eldership (a common result of refusing to submit to the Lordship of Christ), they may experience an increase in knowledge, but they will not grow in love because love only grows in the context of relationships. I wholeheartedly concur with Donald Whitney: "No one develops the proper spiritual symmetry just by listening to Christian radio, watching Christian television, or reading Christian books. You can't get this kind of maturity merely by participating in a group Bible study. Unless you're an active part of a local church, your Christian life and ministry will be imbalanced."21 According to Scripture, "Knowledge makes arrogant, but love edifies" (1 Cor. 8:1). Biblical love is directed toward other people. If there are no "other people," growth becomes imbalanced.

In contrast to those who have made a custom of forsaking the local assembly, believers need to continually encourage one another, "and all the more as you see the day drawing near" (Heb. 10.25). The day referred to here is probably the destruction of Jerusalem; however, the return of Christ is a legitimate application and provides divine incentive for faithful participation in the community of faith.

It is important to take note of the repeated call "let us" (10:22–24), which emphasizes that these are responsibilities that believers must fulfill together, not alone. All three uses are in the present tense, which means that the writer was encouraging his readers to keep on doing these things. Until Christ returns, or we meet Him in death, there will never be a time when we do not need to be actively involved in a community of the faith that stimulates us toward holiness. We cannot do it alone. H. A. Ironside comments,

The believer is not alone in his confession of Christ, nor is he to act in isolation. He is linked with others both by nature and grace, and he is called upon to seek to stir up his brethren unto love and to good works, assembling with fellow-saints for worship, prayer, and testimony, not coldly withdrawing himself as the manner of some, but remembering his responsibility toward his brethren.[22]

With privilege comes responsibility. Our privileges as New-Covenant believers should compel us each to be faithful to a local assembly of believers in Jesus Christ.

At this point, it is crucial to emphasize the cross-generational, same-gender strategy for discipleship outlined by the Apostle Paul in Titus 2:1–8:

> But as for you, speak the things which are fitting for sound doctrine. Older men are to be temperate, dignified, sensible, sound in faith, in love, in perseverance. Older women likewise are to be reverent in their behavior, not malicious gossips nor enslaved to much wine, teaching what is good, so that they may encourage the young women to love their husbands, to love their children, to be sensible, pure, workers at home, kind, being subject to their own husbands, so that the word of God will not be dishonored. Likewise urge the young men to be sensible; in all things show yourself to be an example of good deeds, with purity in doctrine, dignified, sound in speech which is beyond reproach, so that the opponent will be put to shame, having nothing bad to say about us.

Perhaps the least-used but richest resource in the local church for the ministry of counseling is the older saints. They are God's intended counselors—the key that unlocks the door to cross-generational discipleship.

The "older men" in the church are instructed to be examples of mature godliness (vv. 1–2): temperate, dignified, sensible, sound in faith, in love, and in perseverance. Displaying these qualities enables them to train the younger men to be sensible, examples of good deeds, pure in doctrine, dignified, and self-controlled in speech (vv. 6–8).

The "older women" in the church are also called to be examples of mature godliness: reverent in their behavior, not malicious gossips, self-controlled, disciplined, and teachers of goodness, both publicly by example and privately in word (v. 3). It is crucial to note that the consistent, godly life of the older women becomes the foundation of their ministry. Paul taught that they are to be all this in order "*that* they may encourage the young women." In other words, being comes before doing. Their example was to precede their instruction. In this way, the older women will earn the respect of the younger women in the church, thus paving the way for the eager reception of their verbal instruction, encouragement, and counsel. Mature women model godliness so that they may disciple younger women to be husband-loving and children-loving, sensible, pure, committed to their domestic calling, kind, and submissive to their husbands (vv. 4–5).

This Titus 2 philosophy of cross-generational discipleship clearly implies same-gender counseling. Older men were responsible for discipling younger men, and older women were responsible for training younger women. This understanding is effectively defended by Carol Cornish, co-editor of *Women Helping Women*:

> The teaching was to be same-gender because women were to be examples both as faithful Christians and as faithful Christian women for other women. Those who were to teach were to be good examples to those being taught. Therefore, those who were more spiritually mature were to teach and be examples for those of the same sex who were less mature. As you can see, then, God's Word gives us a framework for a discipling ministry to women. While the Bible doesn't talk about a distinct process called "counseling," it does couch counseling-type issues within discussions about ministry and discipling and body life within the church. Thus it seems reasonable to conclude that these principles from Titus still apply in terms of who should disciple/counsel whom. Mature men are to counsel men, and mature women are to counsel women. In any situation where teaching, counseling, discipling is being done on a long-term basis one-to-one, the biblical pattern is for such ministry to be same-gender.[23]

The most effective model for youth discipleship is not the modern paradigm of the youth group, which all too often becomes nothing more than a larger gathering of immature fools, but rather the mentoring of young men and women by means of relationships with older, godly believers within the church. As mature believers model Christlikeness within the body life of the local family of God, younger believers observe examples of faithfulness that will stimulate growth in godliness.

Summary

The church is a body. The church is a family. The church is an assembly of the redeemed linked together; not independent, but interdependent. Therefore, there is no better place for the ministry of counseling than a Christ-centered, cross-driven, faith-stimulating community of the faith. God has equipped, and is equipping, the church with older men and women who model Christlikeness in order to disciple younger men and women to walk in obedience to Him. In spite of its innumerable weaknesses, the church is God's ideal environment for intensely focused personal discipleship. In his book *Spiritual Disciplines Within the Church*, Donald Whitney concludes,

> Jesus Christ is the glory of the church. He loves the church and died for the church (Acts 20:28; Ephesians 5:25). With all of its spots and wrinkles, He is at work in and through the church. Regardless of how you view the general condition of the church today or the state of the individual churches in your area, the ultimate future of the church is glorious beyond imagination. Therefore the potential for joy is greater in the church than is promised to any other earthly entity. As the local church is still comprised of sinners in a fallen world, there's no denying the reality of failure and discord in the church. But with all its faults, because of Christ there is more to enjoy in the church than the world dreams of.[24]

The task of the church is to make disciples of Jesus Christ, those who walk in the obedience of submissive faith. As believers are equipped to demonstrate biblical love by counseling one another toward maturity with the Word of God, their lives will reflect the holiness of Christ, and His name will be glorified before a watching world.

For further thought and small-group discussion

1. Read Acts 2:42. Discuss the priorities of the early church. Why is the term "independent Christian" inconsistent with the biblical model for church life?

2. Read Hebrews 10:19–25. Discuss the Christ-centeredness of biblical fellowship.

3. Read Psalm 51. Discuss the importance of repentance and spiritual cleansing to acceptable worship. Take some time to walk yourself through this psalm, praying it back to God.

4. Read Hebrews 10:24. Discuss the meaning of the word "stimulate." Why does God not want believers to make a habit of missing church? What changes does the Holy Spirit want you to make regarding your involvement in your church?

5. Read Titus 2:1–8. Discuss the various roles of men, women, and youth in the discipleship strategy of the local church. Where do you fit in? How will your life and your ministry be different because of this study?

Conclusion

The Lord of the church is at work. Jesus Christ is building His church. However, He is not only building His church, He is also making her holy—a work that He will not stop performing until she is blameless: "… Christ also loved the church and gave Himself up for her, that He might sanctify her, having cleansed her by the washing of water with the word, so that He might present to Himself the church in all her glory, having no spot or wrinkle or any such thing; but that she would be holy and blameless" (Eph. 5:25–27).

The overall theme and objective of this book is the sanctification of the church. Specifically, it establishes a biblical theology for the work of discipleship which occurs in the context of relationships with other believers. Making disciples of Christ is not merely about leading people to saving faith in Him by means of evangelism, but it also requires a more personal ministry—a coming alongside those who believe, to help them live out the reality of their new position in Christ by learning to walk in obedient faith. This is authentic biblical counseling, and this enabling process is the work of the church.

The Holy Spirit empowers the proclamation of the gospel to regenerate spiritually dead sinners to the call of repentance and to believe in Jesus Christ. Once converted, followers of Christ need the care of committed, nurturing ministers who live the Christian life alongside them, helping them experience spiritual growth. This is God-centered church growth, its success measured by how believers are built up in the faith and conformed to the image of the complete man, Jesus Christ. This kind of growth takes place as the undershepherds of Christ faithfully equip the members of their flocks to counsel one another from the Scriptures.[1]

Biblical ministry is all about helping people live out the truth of Jesus Christ for the glory of God. Carson articulates this conviction: "When we live up to our calling, we remember that in God's church people do not set the agenda, they are the agenda. Our allegiance to God and his gospel will be demonstrated in our service to his people, to those who will become his people, to those made in his image."[2] Commitment to help one another grow in godliness is indispensable to the work of discipleship.

Since practical sanctification is not an instantaneous event, but rather a progressive remolding of one's life, it requires every believer to continually apply personal discipline to his or her thoughts, desires, and habits. This process of becoming holy—living out our righteous position in Christ—has its share of hurdles to overcome. Some believers will stumble; they will need the rescuing ministry of those who love them enough to confront them, so that they may be restored to the intimate fellowship with God that grows from obedience.

To accomplish this work, the Holy Spirit has not left us without adequate equipment. Instead, He inspired Scripture, which is the mind of God in written form, thus leaving us with God's infallible, all-sufficient wisdom for life and godliness. When submitted to, it changes the heart of man and leads to spiritual maturity and fruitfulness. Jesus is so committed to the sanctification of His people that He designed and ordained the ideal context in which this spiritual growth may take place. According to His blueprint, local churches function as living communities of the faith in which those who trust the person and work of Christ for their redemption may worship and serve Him together in sincerity and truth.

In spite of these great provisions, however, today's church has largely turned its ear away from the Word of God and embraced the subtle flattery of a Christianized psychology that exalts self and diminishes the uniqueness, power, and simplicity of the gospel. Authentic biblical counselors find themselves actively engaged in the battle for Truth and must, therefore, combat the philosophies of men using "the sword of the Spirit, which is the word of God" (Eph. 6:17).

The Lord of the church will return for His bride. When He does so, the work of counseling will be complete, for all who know Christ "will be like Him, because we will see Him just as He is" (1 John 3:2). Until then, believers must be trained to walk in the Spirit through submission to His Word. We *must* serve one another in the body of Christ by speaking the truth in love. We *must* counsel one another.

"Now to Him who is able to do exceeding abundantly beyond all that we ask or think, according to the power that works within us, to Him be the glory in the church and in Christ Jesus to all generations forever and ever. Amen" (Eph. 3:20–21).

Endnotes

Foreword

1   This word is not restricted to and "does not mean the delivery of a learned and edifying or hortatory discourse in well-chosen words and a pleasant voice," Gerhard Kittel, Geoffrey W. Bromiley and Gerhard Friedrich, (eds.), Theological Dictionary of the New Testament, vol. iii (electronic edn; Grand Rapids, MI: Eerdmans, 1964–c.1976), p. 703.

Chapter 1

1   Cara Marcano, "Growing Christian Shrinks," in The Wall Street Journal, 30 March 2007; www. opinionjournal.com, accessed 30 March 2007.

2   Ibid.

3   Ibid.

4   George Marsden, Reforming Fundamentalism: Fuller Seminary and the New Evangelicalism (Grand Rapids, MI: Eerdmans, 1987).

5   Harold Lindsell, The Battle for the Bible (Grand Rapids, MI: Zondervan, 1976), pp. 106–107.

6   Marsden, p. 181.

7   Ibid.

8   Ibid.

9   Ibid.

10 Ibid.

11 Ibid.

12 Os Guinness, "America's Last Men and Their Magnificent Talking Cure," in The Journal of Biblical Counseling, 15/2 (1997): 24.

13 Lindsell, The Battle, p. 25.

14 Marsden, Reforming Fundamentalism, p. 203.

15 Lindsell, The Battle, p. 108.

16 Marsden, Reforming Fundamentalism, pp. 205–206.

17 Ibid., p. 207.

18 Ibid., p. 233.

19 Ibid., p. 234.

20 Ibid., p. 235.

21 Ibid.

22 Ibid., p. 236.

23 Ibid.

24 John F. MacArthur, Jr., Our Sufficiency in Christ (Dallas: Word Publishing, 1991), pp. 59–60.

25 W. E Vine, Merrill Unger, and William White, Vine's Complete Expository Dictionary of Old and New Testament Words (Nashville, TN: Thomas Nelson, 1985), p. 62.

26 Fritz Rienecker and Cleon Rogers, A Linguistic Key to the Greek New Testament (Grand Rapids, MI: Zondervan, 1976), p. 571.

27 Ibid.

28 Richard Chenevix Trench, Synonyms of the New Testament (Grand Rapids, MI: Baker, 1989), p. 126.

29 Vine, Unger, and White, Expository Dictionary, p. 13.

30 David Powlison, Seeing with New Eyes (Phillipsburg, NJ: P&R, 2003), p. 1.

31 Warren Wiersbe and David Wiersbe, The Elements of Preaching (Wheaton, IL: Tyndale House, 1986), p. 48.

Chapter 2

1   Well over a decade ago, David Powlison used the word "rediscovery" to describe the return of the church to the ministry of biblical counseling. He explained, "In the nineteenth and twentieth centuries, American Christians basically lost the use of truths and skills they formerly possessed. That is, practical wisdom in the cure of souls waned … The Church lost that crucial component of pastoral skill that can be called case-wisdom—wisdom that knows people, knows how people change, and knows how to help people change" (quoted in John MacArthur and Wayne Mack, (eds.),

Introduction to Biblical Counseling (Dallas: Word Publishing, 1994), p. 44).

2 Bill Hull, *The Disciple Making Pastor* (Grand Rapids, MI: Fleming H. Revell, 1988), p. 19.

3 W. E. Vine, Merrill Unger, and William White, *Vine's Complete Expository Dictionary of Old and New Testament Words* (Nashville, TN: Thomas Nelson, 1985), p. 171.

4 F. Wilbur Gingrich, *Shorter Lexicon of the Greek New Testament* (Chicago: University of Chicago Press, 1957), p. 129.

5 According to the *Theological Dictionary of the New Testament*, of the some 250 times that mathetes [[Greek -Bwygrkl]] occurs in the Gospels and Acts, each instance implies "attachment to a person" (Geoffrey W. Bromiley, (ed.), *Theological Dictionary of the New Testament* (Grand Rapids, MI: Eerdmans, 1985), p. 559).

6 All italicized words or phrases within Scripture quotations indicate emphasis added by this author. Italics within non-Scriptural quotations are the original writer's.

7 Edward Hinson, "Biblical View of Man: The Basis for Nouthetic Confrontation," in *The Journal of Pastoral Practice*, 3/1 (1979): 55–56.

8 Spiros Zodhiates, *The Complete Word Study New Testament* (Chattanooga, TN: AMG Publishers, 1991), p. 933.

9 Robert E. Coleman, *The Master Plan of Evangelism* (Old Tappan, NJ: Fleming H. Revell, 1963), p. 51.

10 Jim Berg, *Changed Into His Image* (Greenville, SC: Bob Jones University Press, 2000), p. 11.

11 W. Robertson Nicoll, (ed.), *The Expositor's Greek Testament: Volume 1* (Grand Rapids, MI: Eerdmans, 1976), p. 339.

12 David M. Doran with Pearson Johnson and Benjamin Eckman, *For the Sake of His Name* (Allen Park, MI: Student Global Impact, 2002), p. 72.

13 Spiros Zodhiates, *Who Is Worth Following?* (Ridgefield, NJ: AMG Publishers, 1976), p. 75.

14 *The New Hampshire Confession of Faith*, 1833.

15 Vine, Unger, and White, *Expository Dictionary*, pp. 525–526.

16 Wayne Grudem, *Systematic Theology* (Grand Rapids, MI: Zondervan, 1994), p. 713.

17 J. Ligon Duncan and Susan Hunt, *Women's Ministry in the Local Church* (Wheaton, IL: Crossway, 2006), pp. 49–50. In Susan Hunt's introduction to the chapter from which this quote is taken, she writes, "This chapter is adapted from a sermon Ligon preached at a women's leadership conference, and I particularly wanted him to include it in this book. The principles are the same for men and women, but it was preached specifically to women. It was electrifying for us as we were challenged to fall in love with the church" (p. 45).

18 Nicoll, *Greek Testament*, p. 340.

19 Fritz Rienecker and Cleon Rogers, *A Linguistic Key to the Greek New Testament* (Grand Rapids, MI: Zondervan, 1976), p. 87.

20 Vine, Unger, and White, *Expository Dictionary*, p. 340.

21 Iain Murray, *Spurgeon v. Hyper-Calvinism* (Edinburgh: Banner of Truth, 1995), p. 9.

22 Coleman, *Master Plan*, p. 56.

23 Charles H. Spurgeon, *An All-Round Ministry* (Pasadena, TX: Pilgrim Publications, 1983), p. 373.

24 A. B. Bruce, *The Training of the Twelve* (Grand Rapids, MI: Kregel Publications, 1988), pp. 536–537.

25 Quoted in David Powlison, "A Nouthetic Philosophy of Ministry: An Interview with Steve Viars," in *The Journal of Biblical Counseling*, 20/3 (2002), pp. 33–34.

Endnotes

Chapter 3

1 Wayne Grudem, *Systematic Theology* (Grand Rapids, MI: Zondervan, 1994), p. 709.

2 Robert Duncan Culver, *Systematic Theology* (Fearn: Mentor/Christian Focus, 2005), p. 699.

3 W. E Vine, Merrill Unger, and William White, *Vine's Complete Expository Dictionary of Old and New Testament Words* (Nashville, TN: Thomas Nelson, 1985), p. 647.

4 Culver, *Systematic Theology*, p. 702.

5 Thomas R. Schreiner, *Paul: Apostle of God's Glory in Christ* (Downers Grove, IL: InterVarsity Press, 2001), p. 103.

6 Charles M. Horne, *The Doctrine of Salvation* (Chicago: Moody Press, 1971), p. 1.

7 Fyodor Dostoevsky, *The Brothers Karamazov* (1879–1880; 2004, New York: Barnes & Noble), p. 221.

8 Millard Erickson, *Christian Theology* (Grand Rapids, MI: Baker, 1983), p. 539.

9 Del Fehsenfeld, Jr., *Ablaze with His Glory* (Nashville, TN: Thomas Nelson, 1993), p. 63.

10 For example: David N. Steele, Curtis C. Thomas, and S. Lance Quinn, (eds.), *The Five Points of Calvinism* (1963; 2004, Phillipsburg, NJ: P&R), p. 19.

11 F. F. Bruce, Paul: *Apostle of the Heart Set Free* (Grand Rapids, MI: Eerdmans, 1977), p. 249.

12 G. Campbell Morgan, *The Corinthian Letters of Paul* (Old Tappan, NJ: Fleming H. Revell, 1946), p. 13.

13 Leon Morris, *1 Corinthians* (Tyndale New Testament Commentaries; Grand Rapids, MI: Eerdmans, 1985), p. 93.

14 Ibid.

15 Vine, Unger, and White, *Expository Dictionary*, p. 252.

16 Joshua Harris, *Not Even a Hint* (Sisters, OR: Multnomah, 2003), p. 26.

17 For example, in my church we regularly use the following resources to help people grow in personal holiness: Jerry Bridges' *The Pursuit of Holiness* and *The Practice of Godliness*, Kent Hughes's *Disciplines of a Godly Man*, numerous booklets published by the Christian Counseling & Educational Foundation (CCEF), Jim Berg's *Changed Into His Image*, Joshua Harris's *Not Even a Hint*, Jay Adams's *Disciplines of Godliness*, and more.

18 Jeff Van Goethem, *Living Together* (Grand Rapids, MI: Kregel Publications, 2005), p. 17.

19 Ibid., p. 85.

20 R. Kent Hughes, *Disciplines of Grace* (Wheaton, IL: Crossway, 1993), pp. 129–130.

21 Helpful resources that my local church uses include Alistair Begg's *Lasting Love*, Wayne Mack's *Strengthening Your Marriage*, Bryan Chapell's *Each For the Other*, Jay Adams's *Christian Living in the Home*, and others.

22 We regularly use the following resources to disciple men and husbands in my local church: Kent Hughes's *Disciplines of a Godly Man*, James MacDonald's *I Want to Change, So Help Me God*, Lou Priolo's *The Complete Husband*, Stuart Scott's *The Exemplary Husband*, Wayne Mack's *Strengthening Your Marriage*, Oswald Sanders' *Spiritual Leadership*, and others.

23 We regularly use the following resources to disciple women and wives in my local church: Barbara Hughes's *Disciplines of a Godly Woman*, Martha Peace's *The Excellent Wife*, Nancy Leigh DeMoss's *Lies Women Believe*, Elizabeth George's *A Woman After God's Own Heart*, and others.

24 We regularly use the following resources to disciple parents in my local church: Ted Tripp's *Shepherding a Child's Heart*, Paul David Tripp's *The Age of Opportunity*, Lou Priolo's *The Heart of Anger* and *Teach Them Diligently*, Crown Financial Ministries' *Handling Finances God's Way*, John MacArthur's *Successful Christian Parenting*, Wayne Mack's *Your Family God's Way*, and others.

25 William Brown, in Baxter, *Reformed Pastor* (1656; 1974, Edinburgh: Banner of Truth), p. 23.

26 Ibid., pp. 100–102.

27 Fritz Rienecker and Cleon Rogers, *A Linguistic Key to the Greek New Testament* (Grand Rapids, MI: Zondervan, 1976), p. 402.

28 Simon J. Kistemaker, *1 Corinthians* (New Testament Commentary; Grand Rapids, MI: Baker, 1993), p. 188.

29 Gordon D. Fee, *The First Epistle to the Corinthians* (NICNT; Grand Rapids, MI: Eerdmans, 1987), p. 244.

30 Rus Walton, *Biblical Solutions to Contemporary Problems* (Brentwood, TN: Wolgemuth & Hyatt, 1988), p. 285.

31 Edward T. Welch, *Homosexuality: Speaking the Truth in Love* (Phillipsburg, NJ: P&R, 2000), p. 37.

32 Strong, James, *Strong's Exhaustive Concordance of the Bible* (Peabody, MA: Hendricksen, n.d.).

33 Schreiner, *Paul*, p. 106.

34 For example, David Powlison, *Seeing with New Eyes* (Phillipsburg, NJ: P&R, 2003), p. 131.

35 For example, Elyse Fitzpatrick, *Idols of the Heart* (Phillipsburg, NJ: P&R, 2001).

36 Richard Chenevix Trench, *Synonyms of the New Testament* (Grand Rapids, MI: Baker, 1989), pp. 171–173.

37 Vine, Unger, and White, *Expository Dictionary*, p. 219.

38 Strong, *Concordance*, #4123.

39 Trench, *Synonyms*, p. 98.

40 Edward T. Welch, *Blame It on the Brain?* (Phillipsburg, NJ: P&R, 1998), p. 191.

41 Ibid., pp. 189–190.

42 Paul David Tripp, "Speaking Redemptively," in David Powlison and William P. Smith, (eds.), *A Selection of Readings: Counsel the Word*

(Glenside, PA: Christian Counseling & Educational Foundation, 2002), pp. 36–45.

43 Richard I. and Richard W. Gregory, *On the Level* (Grandville, MI: IFCA Press, 2005), p. 39.

44 Fee, *The First Epistle to the Corinthians*, p. 248. I do not agree with Fee's doctrinal view, which rejects the eternal security of the believer.

45 John Calvin, *Calvin's Commentaries*, vol. xx (Grand Rapids, MI: Baker, 1998), p. 210.

46 D. A. Carson, *A Call to Spiritual Reformation* (Grand Rapids, MI: Baker, 1992), p. 48.

47 Jay E. Adams, *From Forgiven to Forgiving* (Amityville, NY: Calvary Press, 1994), p. 59.

48 Strong, *Concordance*, #37.

49 Erickson, *Christian Theology*, pp. 967–968.

50 Jim Berg, *Changed Into His Image* (Greenville, SC: Bob Jones University Press, 2000), p. 146.

51 Charles Hodge, *1 & 2 Corinthians* (1857; 1958, Geneva Commentaries; Carlisle, PA: Banner of Truth), p. 99.

52 Jeremiah Burroughs, *Gospel Fear* (1647; 1991, Orlando, FL: Soli Deo Gloria), p. 102.

Chapter 4

1 James Montgomery Boice, *Romans*, vol. ii: *The Reign of Grace* (Grand Rapids, MI: Baker, 1992), pp. 765–766.

2 R. Kent Hughes, *Set Apart* (Wheaton, IL: Crossway, 2003), pp. 9–10.

3 Ibid., pp. 51–52.

4 Ibid., pp. 66–67.

5 Ibid., p. 90.

6 Fritz Rienecker and Cleon Rogers, *A Linguistic Key to the Greek New Testament* (Grand Rapids, MI: Zondervan, 1976), p. 747.

7 Ibid.

8 Kenneth S. Wuest, *First Peter in the Greek New Testament* (Grand Rapids, MI: Eerdmans, 1942), p. 35.

9 Warren W. Wiersbe, *Real Worship* (Nashville, TN: Oliver Nelson, 1986), p. 33.

Endnotes

10 Merrill F. Unger, *Unger's Bible Dictionary* (Chicago: Moody Press, 1957), p. 498.

11 Rienecker and Rogers, *Linguistic Key*, p. 375.

12 Phillips translates it as passive: "Don't let the world around you squeeze you into its own mould" (J. B. Phillips, *New Testament* online at http://www.ccel.org/bible/phillips/JBPNT.htm).

13 Matthew Henry argues for this interpretation in his commentary and translates it as "do not fashion yourselves" (*Matthew Henry's Commentary* (McLean, VA: MacDonald Publishing Co., n.d.), p. 457).

14 John Stott, *Romans: God's Good News for the World* (Downers Grove, IL: InterVarsity Press, 1994), p. 323.

15 Timothy and Barbara Friberg, *Analytical Lexicon to the Greek New Testament* (Bible Works 5.0; Norfolk, VA, (2005).

16 Quoted in Michael Green (ed.), *Illustrations for Biblical Preaching* (Grand Rapids, MI: Baker, 1982), p. 188.

17 Wuest, *First Peter*, p. 37.

18 John F. MacArthur, *The MacArthur Study Bible* (Nashville, TN: Word Bibles, 1997), p. 1924.

19 D. Edmond Hiebert, *James* (Chicago: Moody Press, 1979), p. 223.

20 H. A. Ironside, *Hebrews, James, Peter* (1947; 1984, Neptune, NJ: Loizeaux Brothers), p. 41.

21 Hiebert, *James*, p. 223.

22 Jerry Bridges, *The Practice of Godliness* (Colorado Springs, CO: NavPress, 1983), p. 173.

23 Hiebert, *James*, p. 226.

24 Thomas R. Schreiner, *Paul: Apostle of God's Glory in Christ* (Downers Grove, IL: InterVarsity Press, 2001), p. 258.

25 Hughes, *Set Apart*, p. 18.

26 Rienecker and Rogers, *Linguistic Key*, p. 748.

27 Alva J. McClain, *Romans: The Gospel of God's Grace* (Winona Lake, IN: BMH Books, 1973), pp. 43–44.

28 Wayne Grudem, *1 Peter* (Tyndale New Testament Commentaries; Grand Rapids, MI: Eerdmans, 1988), p. 79.

29 Rienecker and Rogers, *Linguistic Key*, p. 748.

30 Cited by J. Ramsey Michaels, *1 Peter* (Word Biblical Commentary; Dallas: Word Books, 1988), p. 59.

31 Jay E. Adams, *The Christian Counselor's Manual* (Grand Rapids, MI: Zondervan, 1973), pp. 176–216.

32 Wuest, *First Peter*, p. 50.

33 Thomas Watson, *The Mischief of Sin* (Morgan, PA: Soli Deo Gloria, 1994), p. 41.

34 Rienecker and Rogers, *Linguistic Key*, p. 749.

35 Jerry Bridges, *Practice of Godliness*, p. 31.

36 Rienecker and Rogers, *Linguistic Key*, p. 750.

37 Wuest, *First Peter*, pp. 50–51.

38 W. E. Vine, Merrill Unger, and William White, *Vine's Complete Expository Dictionary of Old and New Testament Words* (Nashville, TN: Thomas Nelson, 1985), p. 204.

39 Louis A. Barbieri, *First and Second Peter* (Chicago: Moody Press, 1975), p. 47.

40 Wayne Mack, *Your Family God's Way* (Phillipsburg, NJ: P&R, 1991), p. 100.

41 John Piper, *A Godward Life*, Book 2 (Sisters, OR: Multnomah, 1999), p. 183.

42 Boice, *Romans*, p. 770.

Chapter 5

1 William Goode in John F. MacArthur and Wayne Mack, (eds.), *Introduction to Biblical Counseling* (Dallas: Word, 1994), pp. 301–302.

2 Fritz Rienecker and Cleon Rogers, *A Linguistic Key to the Greek New Testament* (Grand Rapids, MI: Zondervan, 1976), p. 518.

3 W.E. Vine, Merrill Unger, and William White, *Vine's Complete Expository Dictionary of Old and New Testament Words* (Nashville, TN: Thomas Nelson, 1985), p. 642.

4   Thomas Watson, *The Mischief of Sin* (Morgan, PA: Soli Deo Gloria, 1994), p. 20.

5   By "professional counselor," I am referring to those in the fields of psychology and psychiatry who attempt to treat the immaterial part of man, the soul. I am not eliminating the legitimate use of *medical physicians* for the diagnosis and treatment of problems that may truly have an organic, biological cause. The wise counselor may often recommend, and sometimes require, a counselee to go to his or her family practitioner for a complete physical to determine if there may be any physiological contributions to the problem(s). If appropriate tests fail to uncover something that is truly wrong with the body, the biblical counselor can then deal strictly with soul-related problems that need biblical correction. The Bible recognizes the place of true medicine in our lives: Jesus treated the presence of medical doctors as one of the realities of our living in sin-cursed bodies (Matt. 9:12); and the Apostle Paul had a medical doctor, Luke, as his traveling companion and personal attendant (Col. 4:14; 2 Tim. 4:11). However, some illnesses should also induce believers to call their pastor-elders for anointing and prayer, according to the instruction of James 5:13–16, so that the possibility of the presence of a sin-cause can be gently confronted, resulting in biblical confession. The Scriptures warn us not to seek the help of physicians *in place of* seeking help from the Lord (2 Chr. 16:12). If a counselee is seeking help from the Lord through biblical counseling, there is no reason for him or her not to be a wise steward of the vast medical knowledge that God has blessed us with, provided it does not become a mask that diminishes the reality of spiritual problems of the heart.

6   Dr. Paul Brand and Philip Yancey, *Fearfully and Wonderfully Made* (Grand Rapids, MI: Zondervan, 1980), p. 91.

7   Vine, Unger, and White, *Expository Dictionary*, p. 594.

8   Paul David Tripp, "Speaking Redemptively," in David Powlison and William P. Smith, (eds.), *A Selection of Readings: Counsel the Word* (Glenside, PA: Christian Counseling & Educational Foundation, 2002), p. 45.

9   William F. Arndt and F. Wilbur Gingrich, *A Greek–English Lexicon of the New Testament* (Chicago: University of Chicago Press, 1957), p. 134.

10 Richard Baxter, *The Reformed Pastor* (1656; 1974, Edinburgh: Banner of Truth), pp. 98–99.

11 Jay E. Adams, *The Christian Counselor's Manual* (Grand Rapids, MI: Zondervan, 1973), p. 141.

Chapter 6

1   Bill Hull, *The Disciple Making Pastor* (Grand Rapids, MI: Fleming H. Revell, 1988), p. 42.

2   Henry C. Thiessen, *Lectures in Systematic Theology* (Grand Rapids, MI: Eerdmans, 1949), p. 65.

3   Wayne Grudem, *Systematic Theology* (Grand Rapids, MI: Zondervan, 1994), pp. 74–75.

4   William F. Arndt and F. Wilbur Gingrich, *A Greek–English Lexicon of the New Testament* (Chicago: University of Chicago Press, 1957), p. 900.

5   Ibid., p. 249.

6   Fritz Rienecker and Cleon Rogers, *A Linguistic Key to the Greek New Testament* (Grand Rapids, MI: Zondervan, 1976), p. 647.

7   Richard Chenevix Trench, *Synonyms of the New Testament* (Grand Rapids, MI: Baker, 1989), pp. 125–126.

8   Ibid., p. 126.

9   Curtis C. Thomas, *Life in the Body of Christ* (Cape Coral, FL: Founders Press, 2006), p. 103.

10 Arndt and Gingrich, *Lexicon*, p. 110.

11 Trench, *Synonyms*, p. 91.

Endnotes

12 Quoted in Iain Murray, *Spurgeon v. Hyper-Calvinism* (Edinburgh: Banner of Truth, 1995), p. 7.

13 Quoted in Iain Murray, *Jonathan Edwards: A New Biography* (Edinburgh: Banner of Truth, 1987), p. 243.

14 Strong, James, *Strong's Exhaustive Concordance of the Bible* (Peabody, MA: Hendricksen, n.d.), #2198.

15 A. W. Tozer, *The Pursuit of God* (Camp Hill, PA: Christian Publications, 1982), p. 74.

16 Rienecker and Rogers, *Linguistic Key*, p. 676.

17 Strong, *Concordance*, #5114.

18 Quoted in Warren Wiersbe, (ed.), *Prokope*, July–September 1997.

19 Arndt and Gingrich, *Lexicon*, p. 453.

20 A. W. Pink, *The Attributes of God* (Grand Rapids, MI: Baker, 1975), p. 23.

21 Jerry Bridges, *Transforming Grace* (Colorado Springs, CO: NavPress, 1991), pp. 177–179.

22 Strong, *Concordance*, #1897.

23 Quoted in Doug Phillips, (ed.), *The Bible Lessons of John Quincy Adams* (San Antonio, TX: Vision Forum, 2002), p. 14.

24 D. Martyn Lloyd-Jones, *Spiritual Depression: Its Causes and Cure* (Grand Rapids, MI: Eerdmans, 1965), pp. 20–21.

25 Donald S. Whitney, *Spiritual Disciplines for the Christian Life* (Colorado Springs, CO: NavPress, 1991), p. 42.

26 Jeremiah Burroughs, *Gospel Fear* (1647; 1991; Orlando, FL: Soli Deo Gloria), pp. 10–11.

Chapter 7

1 Mal Couch, *A Biblical Theology of the Church* (Grand Rapids, MI: Baker, 1999), p. 265.

2 Cited by Fritz Rienecker and Cleon Rogers, *A Linguistic Key to the Greek New Testament* (Grand Rapids, MI: Zondervan, 1976), p. 387.

3 Charles Hodge, *1 & 2 Corinthians* (1857; 1958;

Geneva Commentaries; Carlisle, PA: Banner of Truth), p. 18.

4 Don Matzat, *Christ Esteem* (Eugene, OR: Harvest House, 1990), p. 43.

5 W. E. Vine, Merrill Unger, and William White, *Vine's Complete Expository Dictionary of Old and New Testament Words* (Nashville, TN: Thomas Nelson, 1985), p. 467.

6 Gordon D. Fee, *The First Epistle to the Corinthians* (NICNT; Grand Rapids, MI: Eerdmans, 1987), p. 68.

7 Rienecker and Rogers, *Linguistic Key*, p. 388.

8 William MacDonald, *Believer's Bible Commentary* (Nashville, TN: Thomas Nelson, 1995), p. 1749.

9 David F. Wells, *No Place for Truth* (Grand Rapids, MI: Eerdmans, 1993), p. 101.

10 David Powlison, *Speaking Truth in Love: Counsel in Community* (Winston-Salem, NC: Punch Press, 2005), p. 189.

11 Richard J. Goodrich and Albert L. Lukaszewski, *A Reader's Greek New Testament* (Grand Rapids, MI: Zondervan, 2003), p. 363.

12 Jay E. Adams, "Integration," in *The Journal of Biblical Counseling: CD ROM Version 2.0*, PDF file, no date, p. 4.

13 Simon J. Kistemaker, *1 Corinthians* (New Testament Commentary; Grand Rapids, MI: Baker, 1993), p. 80.

14 Rienecker and Rogers, *Linguistic Key*, p. 391.

15 Ibid.

16 G. Campbell Morgan, *The Corinthian Letters of Paul* (Old Tappan, NJ: Fleming H. Revell, 1946), pp. 48–49.

17 Goodrich and Lukaszewski, *Greek New Testament*, p. 363.

18 Rienecker and Rogers, *Linguistic Key*, p. 391.

19 Leon Morris, *1 Corinthians* (Tyndale New Testament Commentaries; Grand Rapids, MI: Eerdmans, 1985), p. 55.

20 Rienecker and Rogers, *Linguistic Key*, p. 391.

21 Vine, Unger, and White, *Expository Dictionary*, p. 685.

22 Goodrich and Lukaszewski, *Greek New Testament*, p. 364.

23 William F. Arndt and F. Wilbur Gingrich, *A Greek–English Lexicon of the New Testament* (Chicago: University of Chicago Press, 1957), p. 177.

24 Hodge, *1 & 2 Corinthians*, p. 43.

25 Rienecker and Rogers, *Linguistic Key*, p. 392.

26 Goodrich and Lukaszewski, *Greek New Testament*, p. 402.

27 Rienecker and Rogers, *Linguistic Key*, p. 486.

28 Goodrich and Lukaszewski, *Greek New Testament*, p. 402.

29 Wells, *No Place for Truth*, p. 7.

30 James Dobson, *Hide or Seek: How to Build Self-Esteem in Your Child* (Old Tappan, NJ: Fleming H. Revell, 1974), pp. 20–21.

31 Ibid., p. 175.

32 Ibid., p. 160.

33 David Powlison, "Critiquing Modern Integrationists," in *The Journal of Biblical Counseling*, 11/3 (1993): 24.

Chapter 8

1 Joshua Harris, *Stop Dating the Church* (Sisters, OR: Multnomah, 2004), pp. 16–17.

2 David Powlison, *Speaking Truth in Love: Counsel in Community* (Winston-Salem, NC: Punch Press, 2005), pp. 110–116.

3 For example, the mission statement of the Biblical Counseling Center in Arlington Heights, IL states, "The mission of Biblical Counseling Center is to equip the local church to do the work of discipling and counseling for its people, by its people based solely on the sufficiency of Scripture. We accomplish this in a three-fold way through Counseling Training, Counseling Resources and Counseling Services" (www.biblicalcounselingcenter.org).

4 Kent Hughes coined this label in *Disciplines of a Godly Man* (Wheaton, IL: Crossway, 1991), p. 153.

5 D. Edmond Hiebert, *An Introduction to the New Testament*, vol. iii (Chicago: Moody Press, 1962), p. 81.

6 Ibid., p. 84.

7 Fritz Rienecker and Cleon Rogers, *A Linguistic Key to the Greek New Testament* (Grand Rapids, MI: Zondervan, 1976), p. 702.

8 Ibid.

9 Herschel H. Hobbs, *Studies in Hebrews* (Nashville, TN: Sunday School Board of the Southern Baptist Convention, 1954), p. 112.

10 Rienecker and Rogers, *Linguistic Key*, p. 703.

11 William F. Arndt and F. Wilbur Gingrich, *A Greek–English Lexicon of the New Testament* (Chicago: University of Chicago Press, 1957), p. 37.

12 W. E. Vine, Merrill Unger, and William White, *Vine's Complete Expository Dictionary of Old and New Testament Words* (Nashville, TN: Thomas Nelson, 1985), p. 597.

13 John Calvin, *Commentaries on the Epistle of Paul the Apostle to the Hebrews* (Grand Rapids, MI: Baker, 2005), pp. 237–238.

14 Richard J. Goodrich and Albert L. Lukaszewski, *A Reader's Greek New Testament* (Grand Rapids, MI: Zondervan, 2003), p. 498.

15 Rienecker and Rogers, *Linguistic Key*, p. 703.

16 Ibid.

17 Timothy S. Lane and Paul David Tripp, *How People Change* (Winston-Salem, NC: Punch Press, 2006), pp. 75–77.

18 Mark Dever and Paul Alexander, *The Deliberate Church* (Wheaton, IL: Crossway, 2005), p. 111.

19 Vine, Unger, and White, *Expository Dictionary*, p. 252.

20 Rienecker and Rogers, *Linguistic Key*, p. 703.

21 Donald S. Whitney, *Spiritual Disciplines Within*

Endnotes

the Church (Chicago: Moody Press, 1996),
p. 52.

22 H. A. Ironside, *Hebrews, James, Peter* (1947;
1984, Neptune, NJ: Loizeaux Brothers), p. 122.

23 Elyse Fitzpatrick and Carol Cornish (eds.),
Women Helping Women (Eugene, OR: Harvest
House, 1997), pp. 88–89.

24 Whitney, *Spiritual Disciplines Within the
Church*, p. 13.

Conclusion

1 For a full explanation of the pastor's role as
equipper, see my companion book, *Counsel
Your Flock* (Leominster, UK: Day One, 2009;
ISBN: 978-1-84625-154-2).

2 D. A. Carson, *A Call to Spiritual Reformation*
(Grand Rapids, MI: Baker, 1992), p. 65.

Bibliography

Adams, Jay E., *The Christian Counselor's Manual* (Grand Rapids, MI: Zondervan, 1973).

———*Christian Living in the Home* (Phillipsburg, NJ: P&R, 1972).

———*From Forgiven to Forgiving* (Amityville, NY: Calvary Press, 1994).

Armstrong, John, (ed.), *The Coming Evangelical Crisis* (Chicago: Moody Press, 1996).

———*The Compromised Church* (Wheaton, IL: Crossway, 1998).

Arndt, William F., and Gingrich, F. Wilbur, *A Greek–English Lexicon of the New Testament* (Chicago: University of Chicago Press, 1957).

Barbieri, Louis A., *First and Second Peter* (Chicago: Moody Press, 1975).

Baxter, J. Sidlow, *Explore the Book* (Grand Rapids, MI: Zondervan, 1960).

Baxter, Richard, *The Reformed Pastor* (1656; 1974, Edinburgh: Banner of Truth).

Berg, Jim, *Changed Into His Image* (Greenville, SC: Bob Jones University Press, 2000).

Boice, James Montgomery, *Romans*, vol. ii: *The Reign of Grace* (Grand Rapids, MI: Baker, 1992).

Brand, Dr. Paul, and Yancey, Philip, *Fearfully and Wonderfully Made* (Grand Rapids, MI: Zondervan, 1980).

Bridges, Charles, *The Christian Ministry* (1830; 1967, Edinburgh: Banner of Truth).

Bridges, Jerry, *The Practice of Godliness* (Colorado Springs, CO: NavPress, 1983).

———*The Pursuit of Holiness* (Colorado Springs, CO: NavPress, 1978).

———*Transforming Grace* (Colorado Springs, CO: NavPress, 1991).

———*Trusting God* (Colorado Springs, CO: NavPress, 1988).

Bromiley, Geoffrey W., (ed.), *Theological Dictionary of the New Testament* (Grand Rapids, MI: Eerdmans, 1985).

Bruce, A. B., *The Training of the Twelve* (Grand Rapids, MI: Kregel Publications, 1988).

Bruce, F. F., *Paul: Apostle of the Heart Set Free* (Grand Rapids, MI: Eerdmans, 1977).

Burroughs, Jeremiah, *Gospel Fear* (1647; 1991, Orlando, FL: Soli Deo Gloria).

Calvin, John, *Calvin's Commentaries* (Grand Rapids, MI: Baker, 1998).

——*Commentaries on the Epistle of Paul the Apostle to the Hebrews* (Grand Rapids, MI: Baker, 2005).

Carson, D. A., *A Call to Spiritual Reformation* (Grand Rapids, MI: Baker, 1992).

Coleman, Robert E., *The Master Plan of Evangelism* (Old Tappan, NJ: Fleming H. Revell, 1963).

Couch, Mal, *A Biblical Theology of the Church* (Grand Rapids, MI: Baker, 1999).

Culver, Robert Duncan, *Systematic Theology* (Fearn: Mentor/Christian Focus, 2005).

DeMoss, Nancy Leigh, *Lies Women Believe* (Chicago: Moody Press, 2001).

Dever, Mark, *Nine Marks of a Healthy Church* (Wheaton, IL: Crossway, 2004).

——and Alexander, Paul, *The Deliberate Church* (Wheaton, IL: Crossway, 2005).

Deyneka, Peter, *Much Prayer—Much Power* (Grand Rapids, MI: Zondervan, 1958).

Dobson, James, *Hide or Seek: How to Build Self-Esteem in Your Child* (Old Tappan, NJ: Fleming H. Revell, 1974).

Doran, David M., with Johnson, Pearson, and Eckman, Benjamin, *For the Sake of His Name* (Allen Park, MI: Student Global Impact, 2002).

Dostoevsky, Fyodor, *The Brothers Karamazov* (1879–1880; 2004, New York: Barnes & Noble).

Duncan, J. Ligon, and Hunt, Susan, *Women's Ministry in the Local Church* (Wheaton, IL: Crossway, 2006).

Elliff, Tom, *A Passion for Prayer* (Wheaton, IL: Crossway, 1998).

Erickson, Millard, *Christian Theology* (Grand Rapids, MI: Baker, 1983).

Fee, Gordon D., *The First Epistle to the Corinthians* (NICNT; Grand Rapids, MI: Eerdmans, 1987).

Fehsenfeld, Jr., Del, *Ablaze with His Glory* (Nashville, TN: Thomas Nelson, 1993).

Fitzpatrick, Elyse, and Hendricksen, M.D., Laura, *Will Medicine*

Stop the Pain? (Chicago: Moody Press, 2006).

——and Carol Cornish, (eds.), *Women Helping Women* (Eugene, OR: Harvest House, 1997).

Timothy and Barbara Friberg, *Analytical Lexicon to the Greek New Testament* (*Bible Works* 5.0; Norfolk, VA, (2005).

Gallagher, Steve, *At the Altar of Sexual Idolatry* (Dry Ridge, KY: Pure Life Ministries, 2000).

Gingrich, F. Wilbur, *Shorter Lexicon of the Greek New Testament* (Chicago: University of Chicago Press, 1957).

Goodrich, Richard J., and Lukaszewski, Albert L., *A Reader's Greek New Testament* (Grand Rapids, MI: Zondervan, 2003).

Green, Michael, (ed.), *Illustrations for Biblical Preaching* (Grand Rapids, MI: Baker, 1982).

Gregory, Richard I. and Richard W., *On the Level* (Grandville, MI: IFCA Press, 2005).

Gromacki, Robert G., *Stand Perfect in Wisdom* (Grand Rapids, MI: Baker, 1981).

Grudem, Wayne, 1 *Peter* (Tyndale New Testament Commentaries; Grand Rapids, MI: Eerdmans, 1988).

——*Systematic Theology* (Grand Rapids, MI: Zondervan, 1994).

——(ed.), Biblical Foundations for Manhood and Womanhood (Wheaton, IL: Crossway, 2002).

Guinness, Os, "America's Last Men and Their Magnificent Talking Cure," in *The Journal of Biblical Counseling*, 15/2 (1997).

Harris, Joshua, *Not Even a Hint* (Sisters, OR: Multnomah, 2003).

——*Stop Dating the Church* (Sisters, OR: Multnomah, 2004).

Hendricksen, William, *Galatians and Ephesians* (New Testament Commentary; Grand Rapids, MI: Baker, 1967).

Henry, Matthew, *Matthew Henry's Commentary*, vols. i–vi (McLean, VA: MacDonald Publishing Co., n.d.).

Hiebert, D. Edmond, *An Introduction to the New Testament*, vols. i–iii (Chicago: Moody Press, 1962).

——*James* (Chicago: Moody Press, 1979).

Bibliography

——*Second Peter and Jude* (Greenville, SC: Unusual Publications, 1989).

Hinson, Edward, "Biblical View of Man: The Basis for Nouthetic Confrontation," in *The Journal of Pastoral Practice*, 3/1 (1979).

Hobbs, Herschel H., *Studies in Hebrews* (Nashville, TN: Sunday School Board of the Southern Baptist Convention, 1954).

Hodge, Charles, *1 &2 Corinthians* (1857; 1958, Geneva Commentaries; Carlisle, PA: Banner of Truth).

Horne, Charles M., *The Doctrine of Salvation* (Chicago: Moody Press, 1971).

Hughes, Barbara, *Disciplines of a Godly Woman* (Wheaton, IL: Crossway, 2001).

Hughes, R. Kent, *Disciplines of a Godly Man* (Wheaton, IL: Crossway, 1991).

——*Disciplines of Grace* (Wheaton, IL: Crossway, 1993).

——*Set Apart* (Wheaton, IL: Crossway, 2003).

Hull, Bill, *The Disciple Making Church* (Grand Rapids, MI: Fleming H. Revell, 1990).

——*The Disciple Making Pastor* (Grand Rapids, MI: Fleming H. Revell, 1988).

——*Jesus Christ Disciplemaker* (Grand Rapids, MI: Fleming H. Revell, 1984).

Ironside, H. A., *Hebrews, James, Peter* (1947; 1984, Neptune, NJ: Loizeaux Brothers).

Johnson, Eric L., and Jones, Stanton L., (eds.), *Psychology and Christianity: Four Views* (Downers Grove, IL: IVP Academic, 2000).

Kistemaker, Simon J., *1 Corinthians* (New Testament Commentary; Grand Rapids, MI: Baker, 1993).

Kuiper, R. B., *God-Centred Evangelism* (London: Banner of Truth, 1966).

Lane, Timothy S., and Tripp, Paul David, *How People Change* (Winston-Salem, NC: Punch Press, 2006).

Lawson, Steven J., *Famine in the Land* (Chicago: Moody Press, 2003).

Lindsell, Harold, *The Battle for the Bible* (Grand Rapids, MI: Zondervan, 1976).

Lloyd-Jones, D. Martyn, *Christian*

Unity (Grand Rapids, MI: Baker, 1980).

———*Spiritual Depression: Its Causes and Cure* (Grand Rapids, MI: Eerdmans, 1965).

———*What Is an Evangelical?* (Edinburgh: Banner of Truth, 1992).

MacArthur, Jr., John F., *Ephesians* (MacArthur New Testament Commentary; Chicago: Moody Press, 1986).

———*The MacArthur Study Bible* (Nashville, TN: Word Bibles, 1997).

———*Our Sufficiency in Christ* (Dallas: Word, 1991).

———and Wayne Mack, (eds.), *Introduction to Biblical Counseling* (Dallas: Word, 1994).

MacDonald, James, *I Want to Change ... So, Help Me God* (Chicago: Moody Press, 2000).

MacDonald, William, *Believer's Bible Commentary* (Nashville, TN: Thomas Nelson, 1995).

Mack, Wayne, *Your Family God's Way* (Phillipsburg, NJ: P&R, 1991).

Marcano, Cara, "Growing Christian Shrinks," in *The Wall Street Journal*, 30 March 2007; www.opinionjournal.com, accessed 30 March 2007.

Marsden, George, *Reforming Fundamentalism: Fuller Seminary and the New Evangelicalism* (Grand Rapids, MI: Eerdmans, 1987).

Matzat, Don, *Christ Esteem* (Eugene, OR: Harvest House, 1990).

McClain, Alva J., *Romans: The Gospel of God's Grace* (Winona Lake, IN: BMH Books, 1973).

Michaels, J. Ramsey, *1 Peter* (Word Biblical Commentary; Dallas: Word, 1988).

Morgan, G. Campbell, *The Corinthian Letters of Paul* (Old Tappan, NJ: Fleming H. Revell, 1946).

Morris, Leon, *1 Corinthians* (Tyndale New Testament Commentaries; Grand Rapids, MI: Eerdmans, 1985).

Murray, Iain, *Jonathan Edwards: A New Biography* (Edinburgh: Banner of Truth, 1987).

———*Spurgeon v. Hyper-Calvinism* (Edinburgh: Banner of Truth, 1995).

Bibliography

Newell, William R., *Romans: Verse by Verse* (Chicago: Moody Press, 1938).

Nicoll, W. Robertson, (ed.), *The Expositor's Greek Testament* (Grand Rapids, MI: Eerdmans, 1976).

Packer, J. I., *Evangelism and the Sovereignty of God* (Downers Grove, IL: InterVarsity Press, 1961).

Phillips, Doug, (ed.), *The Bible Lessons of John Quincy Adams* (San Antonio, TX: Vision Forum, 2002).

Pink, A. W., *The Attributes of God* (Grand Rapids, MI: Baker, 1975).

Piper, John, *A Godward Life*, Book 2 (Sisters, OR: Multnomah, 1999).

——*Let the Nations Be Glad* (Grand Rapids, MI: Baker, 1993).

——*The Hidden Smile of God* (Wheaton, IL: Crossway, 2001).

——*The Pleasures of God* (Sisters, OR: Multnomah, 2000).

——*When the Darkness Will Not Lift* (Wheaton, IL: Crossway, 2006).

——and Grudem, Wayne, (eds.), *Recovering Biblical Manhood and Womanhood* (Wheaton, IL: Crossway, 1991).

Powlison, David, "A Nouthetic Philosophy of Ministry: An Interview with Steve Viars," in *The Journal of Biblical Counseling*, 20/3 (2002).

——*Power Encounters* (Grand Rapids, MI: Baker, 1995).

——*Seeing with New Eyes* (Phillipsburg, NJ: P&R, 2003).

——*Speaking Truth In Love: Counsel in Community* (Winston-Salem, NC: Punch Press, 2005).

——(ed.), *The Journal of Biblical Counseling on CD-ROM*, Version 2.0. (Glenside, PA: Christian Counseling & Educational Foundation, 1977–2005).

——and Smith, William P., (eds.), *A Selection of Readings: Counsel the Word* (Glenside, PA: Christian Counseling & Educational Foundation, 2002).

Priolo, Lou, *The Heart of Anger* (Amityville, NY: Calvary Press, 1997).

Rienecker, Fritz, and Rogers, Cleon, *A Linguistic Key to the Greek*

New Testament (Grand Rapids, MI: Zondervan, 1976).

Rohrer, Norman, and Deyneka, Jr., Peter, *Peter Dynamite: Twice Born Russian* (Loves Park, IL: Slavic Gospel Association, 2005).

Ryle, J. C., "Expository Thoughts on Matthew 7:21–29," http://www.sermonindex.net/ (accessed March 2008).

——*Thoughts for Young Men* (1886; 2002, Moscow, ID: Charles Nolan Publishers).

Sande, Ken, *The Peacemaker* (Grand Rapids, MI: Baker, 2004).

Sanders, J. Oswald, *Spiritual Leadership* (Chicago: Moody Press, 1967).

——*Spiritual Maturity* (Chicago: Moody Press, 1962).

Schreiner, Thomas R., *Paul: Apostle of God's Glory in Christ* (Downers Grove, IL: InterVarsity Press, 2001).

Shaw, John, *The Character of a Pastor According to God's Heart* (Ligonier, PA: Soli Deo Gloria, 1992).

Smith, Robert D., *The Christian Counselor's Medical Desk Reference* (Stanley, NC: Timeless Texts, 2000).

Souder, Patricia, *Alex Leonovich: A Heart for the Soul of Russia* (Camp Hill, PA: Horizon, 1999).

Spence, H. D. M., (ed.) *The Pulpit Commentary* (Grand Rapids, MI: Eerdmans, 1965).

Spurgeon, Charles H., *An All-Round Ministry* (Pasadena, TX: Pilgrim Publications, 1983).

Steele, David N., Thomas, Curtis C., and Quinn, S. Lance, (eds.), *The Five Points of Calvinism* (1963; 2004, Phillipsburg, NJ: P&R).

Stott, John R. W., *Between Two Worlds* (Grand Rapids, MI: Eerdmans, 1982).

——*Romans: God's Good News for the World* (Downers Grove, IL: InterVarsity Press, 1994).

Strong, James, *Strong's Exhaustive Concordance of the Bible* (Peabody, MA: Hendricksen, n.d.).

Tada, Joni Eareckson, and Estes, Steven, *When God Weeps* (Grand Rapids, MI: Zondervan, 1997).

Bibliography

Thiessen, Henry C., *Lectures in Systematic Theology* (Grand Rapids, MI: Eerdmans, 1949).

Thomas, Curtis C., *Life in the Body of Christ* (Cape Coral, FL: Founders Press, 2006).

Tozer, A. W., *The Pursuit of God* (Camp Hill, PA: Christian Publications, 1982).

Trench, Richard Chenevix, *Synonyms of the New Testament* (Grand Rapids, MI: Baker, 1989).

Tripp, Paul David, *Age of Opportunity* (Phillipsburg, NJ: P&R, 1997).

——*War of Words* (Phillipsburg, NJ: P&R, 2000).

Tripp, Ted, *Shepherding a Child's Heart* (Wapwallopen, PA: Shepherd Press, 1995).

Unger, Merrill F., *Unger's Bible Dictionary* (Chicago: Moody Press, 1957).

Van Goethem, Jeff, *Living Together* (Grand Rapids, MI: Kregel Publications, 2005).

Vaughan, W. Curtis, *The Letter to the Ephesians* (Nashville, TN: Convention Press, 1963).

Vine, W. E., Unger, Merrill, and White, William, *Vine's Complete Expository Dictionary of Old and New Testament Words* (Nashville, TN: Thomas Nelson, 1985).

Walton, Rus, *Biblical Solutions to Contemporary Problems* (Brentwood, TN: Wolgemuth & Hyatt, 1988).

Watson, Thomas, *A Body of Divinity* (1692; 1965, London: Banner of Truth).

——*The Doctrine of Repentance* (1668; 1987, Edinburgh: Banner of Truth).

——*The Mischief of Sin* (Morgan, PA: Soli Deo Gloria, 1994).

Webster, Douglas D., *Selling Jesus* (Downers Grove, IL: IVP, 1992).

Welch, Edward T., *Addictions: A Banquet in the Grave* (Phillipsburg, NJ: P&R, 2001).

——*Blame It on the Brain?* (Phillipsburg, NJ: P&R, 1998).

——*Homosexuality: Speaking the Truth in Love* (Phillipsburg, NJ: P&R, 2000).

Wells, David F., *No Place for Truth* (Grand Rapids, MI: Eerdmans, 1993).

Whitney, Donald S., *Spiritual Disciplines for the Christian*

Life (Colorado Springs, CO: NavPress, 1991).

——*Spiritual Disciplines Within the Church* (Chicago: Moody Press, 1996).

Wiersbe, Warren, *Real Worship* (Nashville, TN: Oliver Nelson, 1986).

——(ed.), *Prokope*, July–September 1997.

——and Wiersbe, David, *The Elements of Preaching* (Wheaton, IL: Tyndale House, 1986).

Wuest, Kenneth S., *Wuest's Word Studies: Ephesians* (Grand Rapids, MI: Eerdmans, 1953).

——*First Peter in the Greek New Testament* (Grand Rapids, MI: Eerdmans, 1942).

——*The New Testament: An Expanded Translation* (Grand Rapids, MI: Eerdmans, 1961).

Zodhiates, Spiros, *The Complete Word Study New Testament* (Chattanooga, TN: AMG Publishers, 1991).

——*Who Is Worth Following?* (Ridgefield, NJ: AMG Publishers, 1976).

Soon to be available from www.dayone.co.uk

COUNSEL ONE ANOTHER: ISSUES IN FOCUS

Additional resources from Paul Tautges will soon be available from the Day One website, www.dayone.co.uk. Topics will include:

- Releasing the grip of anxiety
- Getting to the heart of conflict
- Conquering sinful anger
- Taming the wild tongue
- Trusting God in trials

Geared towards small-group study as well as one-on-one counseling relationships, these text and audio downloads will be available to purchase during the course of 2009.

For more details, check out www.dayone.co.uk or, for customers in North America, www.dayonebookstore.com.